THINK-THIN
ONE-POT MEALS

RUTH GLICK

GRAMERCY BOOKS
New York

This 2002 edition is published by Gramercy Books™, an imprint of Random House Value Publishing, Inc., 280 Park Avenue, New York, NY 10017, by arrangement with Surrey Books, Inc.

Gramercy Books™ and design are trademarks of Random House Value Publishing, Inc.

Random House
New York • Toronto • London • Sydney • Auckland
http://www.randomhouse.com/

Printed and bound in the United States of America

[Originally published as *Skinny One-Pot Meals* by Surrey Books, 1997.]

Library of Congress Cataloging-in-Publication Data

Glick, Ruth, 1942-
    Think-thin one-pot meals / Ruth Glick.
        p. cm. – (Think-thin (Series))
    Previous eds. published under title: Skinny one-pot meals.
    Includes index.
    ISBN 0-517-22074-1 (alk. paper)
      1. Casserole cookery. 2. Low-fat diet–Recipes. 3. Cookery, International. I. Glick,
Ruth, 1942-. Skinny one-pot meals. II. Title. III. Series.

TX693 .G58 2002
641.8'21—dc21

2001054321

10 9 8 7 6 5 4 3 2 1

CONTENTS

1
A WEALTH OF ONE-POT MEALS

In these pages you'll find soups, stews, skillet dinners, microwave casseroles, Crock-Pot meals, even one-dish salads. Many are cooked from the beginning in one pot. Others feature a meat and vegetable sauce to be served over pasta, potatoes, rice, or another grain. Most dishes include beef, chicken, turkey, ham, pork, or seafood. But there are also some vegetable and vegetarian selections that rely on tasty and filling combinations of vegetables, grains, and dairy products.

As you thumb through the recipes, you'll notice that they emphasize certain cuts of meat and poultry. For example, in beef dishes the meat is invariably ground round, round steak, flank steak, or lean stew beef. And the poultry called for is chicken or turkey breast. That is because one of the easiest ways to trim fat from your diet is to select only lean cuts of meat and poultry, and to remove all visible fat before cooking.

You may not realize it, but there's a tremendous difference in the fat content of various cuts. A three-ounce portion of untrimmed rib roast has 27 grams of fat, for example. (That's more than a third of your daily recommended fat intake for the day—even if you're a construction worker.) The same amount of well-trimmed lean top round contains only a modest 4.9 grams. (For more information on cuts of meat and poultry, see the introductions to the appropriate chapters.)

Another easy way to trim fat is to switch to reduced-fat or fat-free dairy products. All the ricotta cheese, yogurt, "sour cream", and milk used in *Think-Thin One-Pot Meals*. are reduced-fat or fat-free versions. The reduced-fat mayonnaise has only 5 grams of fat per tablespoon. The only dairy exception is cheese. While I do use reduced-fat varieties in many recipes, sometimes I call for a few ounces of full-fat cheese when it will make a difference in taste of the finished dish.

Which brings me to an important point. Taste is the bottom line in *Think-Thin One-Pot Meals*. Over the years, I've discovered that no matter how nutritious a meal is, it's a waste of effort to cook it if nobody wants to eat it. So you'll find that I do use enough fat in my recipes to provide the richness and eating satisfaction of "real food."

Seasonings are particularly important in lower-fat cooking because fat is not relied upon to give food flavor. Remove it, and you must experiment to find out how to compensate for flavor with other elements. For example, a reduced-fat "cream sauce" may need wine and spices to make it seem creamy. And reduced-fat cheese tastes best when combined with a spicy salsa or picante sauce. Each dish presents its own challenges. Which herbs and spices will bring out the flavor? Do they need to be enhanced with a vinegar? A fruit juice? Another flavor enhancer?

Finding the magic combinations that make food taste rich and satisfying is the thing I like best about reduced-fat cooking. These recipes, I believe, achieve that goal.

As one of my guests said at a recent recipe testing, "If you slipped these dishes in among the high-fat choices at a typical buffet, I wouldn't know they were supposed to be good for me—because they taste so darn good."

That's the kind of comment I love to hear. It validates the philosophy that's kept me testing and retesting recipes for the many nutrition-oriented cookbooks I've written.

About the Recipes

In *Think-Thin One-Pot Meals*, I've mostly used readily available, fresh ingredients. However, I do call for a few specialty items such as rice sticks, sesame oil, and fermented black beans that add flavor and texture to ethnic dishes. Also, for convenience and ease of preparation, I make selected use of prepared items such as tomato sauce, frozen corn and chopped spinach, commercial salsa, and canned chilies.

Utensils and equipment are kept to a minimum. You can make most of the dishes in this book using a Dutch oven or similar heavy pot, a large non-stick skillet, and a couple of casseroles. Or get out your Crock-Pot or other slow cooker and try some of the recipes in Chapter 6.

All of the cooking techniques are easy. However, some may be a little different from the way you're used to doing things since they're specifically designed to trim fat from recipes. For example, I often brown meat under the broiler instead of with oil in a pot on top of the stove. This not only helps to hold the fat in the recipe to 30 percent or less of calories but it's also quick and easy. One of my other favorite fat-reducing techniques is to add a little chicken broth when I'm sauteing vegetables; this reduces the amount of fat needed.

Often, directions call for skimming the fat from soups or gravies using a large, shallow spoon. Don't skip this very simple step because it can remove considerable fat before serving. Also, defat chicken broth by skimming fat off the top before using.

In addition to lowering fat, the recipes are designed to keep sodium to a minimum. Table salt is almost always an optional ingredient, so the recipes can fit into a low-salt diet. The same is true of the reduced-sodium ingredients called for, such as canned tomatoes or tomato sauce. Use them if your physician has told you to restrict sodium or if you prefer to limit salt intake. Otherwise, select the regular versions.

A number of the recipes use a microwave—either to save time, reduce fat in a recipe, or simplify the preparation of classic dishes such as polenta and risotto. My microwave has 900 watts of power, so it cooks very quickly. If yours has less power—or more—you may need to adjust microwaving times somewhat.

Every recipe in *Think-Thin One-Pot Meals* has been tested at least three times not only to ensure that the directions are clear and easy to follow but also that the dish delivers all the taste appeal and satisfaction you deserve.

Using the Nutritional Analyses

Every recipe includes a nutritional analysis done by a registered dietitian using the latest professional nutritional analysis software. You can see at a glance exactly how many calories and how much fat, saturated fat, cholesterol, sodium, protein, and carbohydrates are in each serving—along with the percentage of calories from fat.

Remember that the nutritional analyses are not infallible. Many factors can affect their accuracy: variability in the size of produce; variability in weights and measures; a plus or minus 20 percent error factor in labeling prepared foods; and variations in personal cooking methods.

Where a range of serving sizes is given, the analysis is based on the larger number of servings. When a choice of ingredients is given (for example, chicken broth *or* vegetable broth; reduced-sodium canned tomatoes *or* regular canned tomatoes), the analysis is based on the first choice. If a quantity range is given (for example, ½-¾ cup salsa), the analysis is based on the first number. Optional, "to taste," and ingredients identified as garnishes are not included in the analyses.

2
MEATS

It's quite possible—even *easy*—to stay within the recommended healthy eating guidelines of two or three ounces of lean meat per meal and still feel completely satisfied when you get up from the table. Try some of the recipes in this chapter—Beef Stroganoff, Beef Stew with Rosemary, or Austrian Pork Loin with Apples and Cranberry Sauce—that combine meat with other flavorful and filling ingredients such as grains, beans, vegetables, and fruits. Many, like Middle Eastern Beef and Bean Hot Pot and Polenta with Ham and Peppers, will introduce you to the hearty ethnic dishes of other cultures. But there are also plenty of down-home choices: Scalloped Ham and Potatoes, Round Steak and Roasted Vegetables, and Shepherd's Pie.

Incidentally, high-fat cuts of meat have two or three times as much fat as leaner cuts. So these recipes emphasize the best fat bargains—beef round, flank steak, pork loin, and leg of lamb.

To give you an idea of the fat savings: Three ounces of well-trimmed pork tenderloin contain only 4 grams of fat. Pork spare ribs have 25 grams for the same size serving. Or compare Canadian bacon, which is smoked loin, to regular bacon. The former has 7.1 grams of fat for a 3-ounce portion compared to an astronomical 41.8 for the latter.

BEEF STEW WITH ROSEMARY

For a tasty variation on a popular theme, try this stew, flavored with a kiss of rosemary in addition to thyme and bay leaf. To simplify preparation and eliminate the oil ordinarily used in browning, directions call for coating the beef cubes with flour and browning them under the broiler.

5-6 Servings

1 cup finely chopped onion
1 large garlic clove, minced
2 teaspoons olive oil
1¾ cups defatted chicken broth, divided
1 lb. lean stew beef, trimmed of all fat and cut into small bite-sized pieces
1½ tablespoons white flour
½ cup dry sherry *or* white wine
1 15-oz. can tomato sauce
2 large carrots, peeled and sliced
2 large celery stalks, sliced
3 cups 2-in.-long fresh green bean pieces *or* frozen green beans
1 teaspoon dried rosemary leaves
¼ teaspoon dried thyme leaves
1 large bay leaf
1 teaspoon granulated sugar
¼ teaspoon salt, or to taste (optional)
¼ teaspoon black pepper
1½ cups uncooked white rice, cooked according to package directions

In a Dutch oven, combine onion, garlic, olive oil, and 3 tablespoons broth. Cook, stirring, over medium heat, about 5 or 6 minutes or until onion is tender. If liquid begins to evaporate, add a bit more broth.

Meanwhile, preheat broiler. Adjust rack about 2 inches from heating element. In a shallow baking pan, sprinkle flour over meat. Stir to coat. Spread out pieces so they are separated from one another. Broil about 6 to 7 minutes, turning once or twice, until meat is browned on all sides.

Add remaining broth to Dutch oven, along with sherry and tomato sauce. Stir to mix well. Stir in browned beef cubes. Add carrots, celery, and green beans. Stir in rosemary, thyme, bay leaf, sugar, salt, if desired, and pepper.

Bring to a boil. Cover, reduce heat, and simmer 1½ hours, stirring occasionally, or until vegetables and meat are tender. Remove bay leaf. Remove cover during last 15 minutes of cooking, raise heat to medium, and cook down sauce slightly, stirring occasionally. Serve over white rice.

Nutritional Data (based on 6 servings)

PER SERVING		EXCHANGES	
Calories	395	Milk	0.0
Fat (gm)	5.8	Veg.	3.0
Sat. Fat (gm)	1.7	Fruit	0.0
Cholesterol (mg)	47.3	Bread	3.0
Sodium (mg)	534	Meat	2.0
Protein (gm)	25.6	Fat	0.0
Carbohydrate (gm)	54.9		
% Calories from fat	13		

HUNGARIAN-STYLE BEEF STEW

A good beef stew needs long, slow cooking—unless you make it in the microwave. This rich-tasting Hungarian-style version takes only 20 to 25 minutes, making a rich gravy as it simmers. Incidentally, the recipe was tested with a high-powered (900 w.) microwave. If yours has less power, longer microwaving time may be required.

5-6 Servings

1 cup finely chopped onion
1 large garlic clove, minced
1½ cups reduced-sodium defatted beef broth *or* regular beef broth, divided
1 lb. top beef round steak, trimmed of all fat and cut into small strips
½ cup red Burgundy wine
1 15-oz. can tomato sauce
2 large carrots, peeled and sliced
2 large celery stalks, sliced
1 lb. boiling potatoes, cut into ¾-in. cubes (about 3¼ cups)
1 teaspoon dried thyme leaves
1 teaspoon paprika
¼ teaspoon dry mustard
1 large bay leaf
¼ teaspoon black pepper
½ cup non-fat sour cream
Salt to taste (optional)

In a 3-qt. microwave-safe casserole, combine onion, garlic, and 3 tablespoons broth. Cover and microwave on high power 6 or 7 minutes or until onion is softened, stirring contents and turning casserole once during microwaving.

Preheat broiler. Adjust rack about 2 inches from heating element. In a shallow baking pan, spread out round steak pieces so they are separated from one another. Broil about 5 to 7 minutes, turning once or twice, until meat is browned on all sides.

Add remaining broth to casserole along with wine. Stir in tomato sauce until well combined. Stir in browned beef pieces. Add carrots, celery, and potatoes. Stir in thyme, paprika, mustard, bay leaf, and pepper.

Cover and microwave on high power a total of 20 to 25 minutes or until vegetables and meat are tender. Stir contents and turn casserole one-quarter turn after 8, 12, and 15 minutes. Remove bay leaf. Stir in sour cream. Taste gravy and add salt, if desired.

Nutritional Data (based on 6 servings)

PER SERVING		EXCHANGES	
Calories	217	Milk	0.0
Fat (gm)	2.9	Veg.	1.0
Sat. Fat (gm)	0.9	Fruit	0.0
Cholesterol (mg)	36.5	Bread	1.0
Sodium (mg)	525	Meat	2.0
Protein (gm)	19.1	Fat	0.0
Carbohydrate (gm)	26.9		
% Calories from fat	12		

MIDDLE EASTERN BEEF AND BEAN HOT POT

If you think of beans and rice as primarily a Latin American combination, think again. Here's another delicious, and very different, interpretation.

6 Servings

- 1 cup dried Great Northern beans, washed and sorted
- 1 lb. lean stew beef, cut into small bite-sized pieces
- 2 cups chopped onion
- 2 large garlic cloves, minced
- 2 teaspoons olive oil
- 5 cups defatted beef broth *or* bouillon, divided
- 1 teaspoon dried thyme leaves
- ¼ teaspoon ground cinnamon
- 2 large bay leaves
- ¼ teaspoon black pepper
- 1¼ cups uncooked long-grain white rice
- 1½ cups peeled, diced fresh tomatoes
  Parsley sprigs for garnish (optional)

In a Dutch oven or similar large, heavy pot, cover beans with 2 inches of water. Bring to a boil and boil 2 minutes. Remove from heat and let stand 1 hour. Drain beans in a colander, discarding water. Set beans aside.

Preheat broiler. Adjust rack about 3 inches from heating element. In shallow baking pan, spread out pieces of meat, separated from one another. Broil about 7 to 9 minutes, turning once or twice, until meat is browned on all sides.

Meanwhile, in pot in which beans were cooked, combine onion, garlic, oil, and 3 tablespoons of broth. Cook over medium heat, stirring occasionally, until onion is tender, about 6 or 7 minutes. If liquid begins to evaporate, add more broth.

Add browned meat, beans, thyme, cinnamon, bay leaves, pepper, and remaining broth. Bring to a boil. Cover and simmer 1¼ hours or until beans are partially cooked. With a large, shallow spoon, skim any fat from surface of broth.

Stir in rice and tomatoes. Cover and bring to a boil. Reduce heat and cook an additional 25 minutes or until beans and rice are tender. Remove and discard bay leaves.

Transfer food to a large serving platter. Garnish with parsley sprigs if desired.

Nutritional Data (based on 6 servings)

PER SERVING		EXCHANGES	
Calories	427	Milk	0.0
Fat (gm)	8.1	Veg.	2.0
Sat. Fat (gm)	4.4	Fruit	0.0
Cholesterol (mg)	71	Bread	3.0
Sodium (mg)	595	Meat	3.0
Protein (gm)	35	Fat	0.0
Carbohydrate (gm)	52		
% Calories from fat	17		

BEEF STROGANOFF

When non-fat sour cream came on the market, I was sure it couldn't substitute for the real thing. However, I've found that when used as a sauce ingredient, it can impart a remarkably rich and creamy taste and texture—as it does in this sumptuous Beef Stroganoff. Some brands are better than others, so experiment to find out which you like best.

5-7 Servings

- 1 lb. beef top round, trimmed of all fat
- 1 large onion, finely chopped
- ½ lb. fresh mushrooms, washed, trimmed, and sliced
- 2 large garlic cloves, minced
- 2 teaspoons non-diet, tub-style margarine *or* butter
- 2 cups defatted beef broth, divided
- ¼ cup red Burgundy wine
- 3 tablespoons tomato paste
- ¼ cup water
- 1 tablespoon white flour
- 2 teaspoons granulated sugar
- 1 teaspoon dried thyme leaves
- 1 teaspoon prepared horseradish
- 1 large bay leaf
- ¼ teaspoon black pepper
- ¼ teaspoon salt, or to taste (optional)
- ¾ cup non-fat sour cream

To Serve

- 1½ cups uncooked long-grain white rice *or* 10-12 ozs. uncooked medium non-fat noodles
- Parsley sprigs for garnish (optional)

Cut meat into very thin 2-inch-long diagonal strips.

In a large non-stick, spray-coated skillet, cook meat over medium-high heat 6 or 7 minutes or until browned. Remove meat to a medium bowl and reserve.

In skillet, combine onion, mushrooms, garlic, margarine, and 3 tablespoons broth. Cook over medium heat, stirring, 6 to 7 minutes or until onion is tender and mushrooms have changed color. If liquid begins to evaporate, add more broth.

Return meat to skillet, along with remaining broth and wine. Stir in tomato paste until well combined. Bring to a boil. In a cup, stir flour into water. Add to skillet and cook, stirring, until liquid thickens.

Add sugar, thyme, horseradish, bay leaf, pepper, and salt, if desired, and stir to mix well. Cover and simmer 30 minutes, stirring occasionally, or until meat is tender.

Meanwhile, cook rice or noodles according to package directions.

Reduce heat under skillet so that liquid does not boil. Stir sour cream into broth. Heat 2 or 3 minutes more.

Serve individual portions of Beef Stroganoff over rice or noodles, or arrange rice on a serving platter and top with Beef Stroganoff. Garnish with parsley sprigs if desired.

Nutritional Data (based on 7 servings)

PER SERVING		EXCHANGES	
Calories	336	Milk	0.0
Fat (gm)	6	Veg.	1.0
Sat. Fat (gm)	2	Fruit	0.0
Cholesterol (mg)	55	Bread	2.5
Sodium (mg)	242	Meat	2.5
Protein (gm)	24	Fat	0.0
Carbohydrate (gm)	44		
% Calories from fat	16		

ROUND STEAK AND ROASTED VEGETABLES

The wonderfully crisp potatoes that come along with an oven roast are the best part of the meal. Here's an easy dish that duplicates their flavor and texture—and adds several other favorite vegetables. Instead of a roast, this recipe includes strips of round steak, cut diagonally for tenderness.

6 Servings

1 lb. beef round steak, trimmed of all fat and cut on the diagonal into thin, 3-inch-long strips

3 tablespoons defatted beef broth or beef bouillon (or more if needed)

1 tablespoon canola or safflower oil

4 medium yellow onions, peeled and quartered, or 12 small whole onions

4 medium baking potatoes, peeled and cut into 1¼-inch pieces (1¾ lbs.)

3 medium carrots, peeled and cut into ½- to ¾-inch slices

2 garlic cloves, sliced

½ teaspoon (generous) dried thyme leaves

¼ teaspoon salt (optional)

⅛ teaspoon black pepper

1 medium zucchini, cut into ¼-inch slices

Preheat oven to 350° F.

In large, shallow roasting pan, spread out pieces of meat so they are separated from one another. Roast 10 to 15 minutes, stirring once or twice, until meat is browned on all sides.

Remove pan from oven. Add broth, along with oil, onions, potatoes, carrots, and garlic. Stir to mix well. Sprinkle with thyme, salt, if desired, and pepper. Stir to coat. Return pan to oven, and roast an additional 45 minutes, stirring occasionally.

If vegetables and meat seem dry, add a bit more bouillon. Stir in zucchini and roast an additional 10 to 20 minutes, stirring once, until potatoes are tender and have begun to brown.

Nutritional Data

PER SERVING		EXCHANGES	
Calories	323	Milk	0.0
Fat (gm)	6.9	Veg.	2.0
Sat. Fat (gm)	1.7	Fruit	0.0
Cholesterol (mg)	68	Bread	1.5
Sodium (mg)	65	Meat	3.0
Protein (gm)	31	Fat	0.0
Carbohydrate (gm)	34		
% Calories from fat	19		

BEEF AND TOMATO STIR-FRY

Here's a simple but very appealing beef and tomato dish. Cutting the flank steak diagonally will help tenderize the meat. If flank steak is unavailable, substitute round steak. The five-spice powder and brown sauce called for are frequently used oriental seasonings that can be found in specialty food markets and some grocery stores.

4-5 Servings

1 cup uncooked long-grain white rice

Marinade and Beef

¾ lb. beef flank steak
3 tablespoons dry sherry
2 tablespoons reduced-sodium soy sauce
1 teaspoon five-spice powder
1½ teaspoons rice vinegar
¼ teaspoon ground ginger
Dash black pepper
2-3 drops hot oil (optional)
1 tablespoon cornstarch

Sauce and Vegetables

2 large fresh tomatoes
1 tablespoon sesame oil
1 medium yellow or white onion, sliced
into rings
¾ cup defatted reduced-sodium chicken broth *or* regular defatted chicken broth, divided

1 tablespoon brown sauce
2 teaspoons rice vinegar
1 8-oz. can sliced water chestnuts, drained
2 tablespoons chopped green onion
¼ teaspoon salt, or to taste (optional)
   Additional sliced green onion tops for garnish
   (optional)

Cook rice according to package directions.

Marinade and Beef: With sharp knife, cut flank steak diagonally into thin strips, trimming away and discarding all visible fat.

In medium bowl, mix together sherry, soy sauce, five-spice powder, vinegar, ginger, pepper, and hot oil, if desired. Stir to mix well. Add cornstarch and stir to incorporate thoroughly. Add beef and stir to coat well. Set aside 15 to 20 minutes, stirring occasionally.

Sauce and Vegetables: While beef is marinating, remove skins from tomatoes easily by filling a Dutch oven or large saucepan with about 5 inches of water. Bring to a boil over high heat. When water boils, add tomatoes and cook 1 minute, stirring. Remove tomatoes from boiling water, and place in colander under cold running water. When tomatoes are cool enough to handle, pull off skin and discard. Core and chop tomatoes, and set aside in medium bowl.

Combine sesame oil, onion, and 2 tablespoons broth in large, non-stick skillet. Cook over medium heat, stirring frequently, until onion is almost tender, 4 or 5 minutes. Remove beef from marinade with slotted spoon and add to skillet. Cook, stirring, until beef is browned, about 2 to 3 minutes. Add remaining marinade to skillet along with remaining broth. Raise heat and cook, stirring, until mixture has thickened slightly and boils.

Stir in brown sauce and vinegar. Add tomato pieces, water chestnuts, green onion, and salt, if desired. Bring to a simmer. Lower heat and simmer 2 minutes or until tomato is slightly cooked. Serve beef mixture over rice. Garnish with additional chopped green onion tops, if desired.

Nutritional Data (based on 5 servings)

PER SERVING		EXCHANGES	
Calories	371	Milk	0.0
Fat (gm)	10.1	Veg.	2.0
Sat. Fat (gm)	3.4	Fruit	0.0
Cholesterol (mg)	46	Bread	2.0
Sodium (mg)	284	Meat	2.5
Protein (gm)	23	Fat	0.5
Carbohydrate (gm)	44		
% Calories from fat	25		

SHEPHERD'S PIE

————◆————

Kids and adults love this robust beef stew baked under a mashed potato topping. A small amount of reduced-fat Cheddar cheese adds character to the topping.

6-7 Servings

1 lb. beef round steak
1 large onion, finely chopped
1 garlic clove, minced
2 teaspoons olive oil
1¼ cups defatted beef broth, divided
1 8-oz. can tomato sauce
2 medium carrots, peeled and thinly sliced
2 celery stalks, thinly sliced
2 cups 2-inch-long fresh green bean pieces, stem ends removed
2 large bay leaves
1 teaspoon dried thyme leaves
½ teaspoon dried marjoram leaves
¼ teaspoon powdered mustard
¼ teaspoon black pepper
¼ teaspoon salt, or to taste (optional)
  Dash cayenne pepper

Topping

4 cups 1-inch cubes, peeled boiling potatoes
¼ cup 1% fat milk (approximate)
⅓ cup non-fat yogurt
1 oz. (¼ cup) grated reduced-fat sharp Cheddar cheese
1 tablespoon non-diet, tub-style margarine *or* butter
½ teaspoon salt, scant, or to taste (optional)
⅛ teaspoon, generous, white pepper

Preheat oven to 350° F.

Filling: Trim off and discard all fat from meat. Cut into very thin 2-inch-long diagonal strips.

In spray-coated Dutch oven or other large oven-proof pot, brown meat over medium-high heat, about 6 or 7 minutes. Remove meat to medium-sized bowl and reserve.

In Dutch oven, combine onion, garlic, oil, and 3 tablespoons broth. Cook over medium heat, stirring, 6 or 7 minutes or until onion is tender. If liquid begins to evaporate, add more broth.

Return meat to pot with onion and garlic.

Stir in tomato sauce and remaining beef broth. Stir in carrots, celery, and green beans. Add bay leaves, thyme, marjoram, mustard, pepper, salt, if desired, and cayenne. Stir to mix well. Bake, covered, 1 hour or until meat is tender.

Topping: Meanwhile, in a large saucepan, combine potatoes and enough water to cover. Cover and bring to a boil over high heat. Lower heat and simmer 15 to 17 minutes or until potatoes are very tender. Drain potatoes well in colander.

Return potatoes to pot in which they were cooked, and add remaining topping ingredients. Mash with potato masher. If mixture seems too stiff to spread, add a bit more milk.

Remove stew from oven and uncover. Drop potato topping by large spoonfuls onto bubbling mixture. Carefully spread out topping with back of large spoon, making attractive peaks.

Return to oven and bake, uncovered, 17 to 20 minutes or until potatoes are heated through and begin to brown.

Nutritional Data (based on 7 servings)

PER SERVING		EXCHANGES	
Calories	363	Milk	0.0
Fat (gm)	9.3	Veg.	2.0
Sat. Fat (gm)	2.9	Fruit	0.0
Cholesterol (mg)	68	Bread	2.0
Sodium (mg)	430	Meat	3.0
Protein (gm)	28	Fat	0.0
Carbohydrate (gm)	43		
% Calories from fat	23		

TAMALE PIE

◆───────────

When I first traveled from Washington, D.C., to Santa Barbara, California, to meet my future mother-in-law, she told me that if I were going to make my husband happy, I'd better learn how to make Tamale Pie. Here's a slimmed-down version of the recipe she shared with me. It's still one of my husband's favorites. It can be made either in the microwave or conventionally, although the tortillas will not be as crisp if the dish is microwaved.

6-8 Servings

1 lb. ground round of beef
1 large onion, finely chopped
1 large green bell pepper, seeded and diced
1 garlic clove, minced
2 15-oz. cans tomato sauce
2 16-oz. cans reduced-sodium *or* regular kidney
   beans, well-drained
1½ cups frozen corn kernels
1 tablespoon chili powder, or to taste
1 teaspoon ground cumin
¼ teaspoon salt (optional)
¼ teaspoon black pepper
   Dash cayenne pepper (optional)
1 9-oz. package 6-inch round corn tortillas

Conventional Method: Preheat oven to 350° F.

In 3-qt. flame-proof, oven-proof casserole, combine ground round, onion, green pepper, and garlic. Cook over medium heat, stirring frequently, until beef has changed color. Remove casserole from burner.

Turn out meat mixture onto large plate lined with paper towels to absorb any excess fat. Return to casserole. Add tomato sauce, kidney beans, corn, chili powder, cumin, salt, if desired, black pepper, and cayenne pepper, if desired. Stir to mix well. Scoop out 5 cups of mixture and reserve in medium-sized bowl.

Lay half the tortillas over mixture remaining in casserole, overlapping and covering entire surface. Add 2½ cups of reserved meat and bean mixture over tortillas, spreading it out with back of large spoon. Lay remaining tortillas over mixture in casserole, overlapping and covering entire surface. Top with remaining meat and bean mixture, spreading it out evenly over tortillas.

Bake, uncovered, 45 to 50 minutes or until sauce begins to bubble and flavors are well blended.

Microwave Method: In 2½-quart microwave-safe casserole, stir together ground round, onion, green pepper, and garlic. Cover and microwave on high power 6 to 8 minutes, stirring meat and breaking it up 1 or 2 times during microwaving, until meat is cooked through. With large spoon, break up any remaining large pieces of meat.

Turn out meat mixture onto large plate lined with paper towels to absorb any excess fat. Return to casserole. Add tomato sauce, kidney beans, corn, chili powder, cumin, salt, if desired, black pepper, and cayenne pepper, if desired.

Stir to mix well. Layer casserole with tortillas as directed above under "conventional method."

Cover with casserole lid and microwave on high power 15 to 17 minutes or until mixture is heated through and flavors are well blended. Allow casserole to rest on flat surface 5 minutes before serving.

Nutritional Data (based on 8 servings)

PER SERVING		EXCHANGES	
Calories	306	Milk	0.0
Fat (gm)	3.5	Veg.	1.0
Sat. Fat (gm)	0.8	Fruit	0.0
Cholesterol (mg)	27.4	Bread	3.0
Sodium (mg)	734	Meat	1.5
Protein (gm)	21.6	Fat	0.0
Carbohydrate (gm)	50.6		
% Calories from fat	10		

GROUND BEEF AND PASTA CASSEROLE

◆

*The microwave makes quick work of this flavorful
ground beef and pasta dish.*

5-6 Servings

2 cups uncooked fusilli *or* other similar pasta
   shape
1 lb. ground round of beef
2 cups finely shredded cabbage
1 large onion, finely chopped
1 large green bell pepper, seeded and chopped
1 garlic clove, minced
1 15-oz. can reduced-sodium tomato sauce *or*
   regular tomato sauce
½ cup ketchup
1 tablespoon apple cider vinegar
1½ tablespoons granulated sugar
1 teaspoon dried thyme leaves
¼ teaspoon powdered mustard
⅛ teaspoon ground cinnamon
¼ teaspoon ground black pepper
¼ teaspoon salt, or to taste (optional)

Cook pasta according to package directions. Rinse and drain in colander.

Meanwhile, in 3-qt. microwave-safe casserole, stir together ground round,
cabbage, onion, green pepper, and garlic. Cover with casserole lid, and
microwave on high power 7 to 9 minutes or until meat is cooked through,
turning casserole one-quarter turn, stirring meat, and breaking it up 1 or 2
times during microwaving. With large spoon, break up any remaining large
pieces of meat.

Turn out meat mixture onto large plate lined with paper towels to absorb
any excess fat. Return to casserole.

Stir in tomato sauce, ketchup, vinegar, sugar, thyme, mustard, cinnamon,
black pepper, and salt, if desired.

Cover with casserole lid and microwave on high power 5 to 6 minutes,
turning casserole one-quarter turn and stirring once during microwaving.

Add cooked pasta. Microwave an additional 2 to 3 minutes, turning casserole one-quarter turn and stirring contents once, until cabbage is tender
and flavors are well blended.

Nutritional Data (based on 6 servings)

PER SERVING		EXCHANGES	
Calories	357	Milk	0.0
Fat (gm)	10.0	Veg.	2.0
Sat. Fat (gm)	3.7	Fruit	0.0
Cholesterol (mg)	47	Bread	2.0
Sodium (mg)	250	Meat	2.0
Protein (gm)	21	Fat	1.0
Carbohydrate (gm)	45		
% Calories from fat	25		

POLENTA AND BEANS CON CARNE

Polenta is a Mediterranean cornmeal dish. Like pasta, it makes the perfect base for a flavorful vegetable or meat sauce. This modern microwave version cuts the fat and makes cooking simple. The recipe was designed using a high-powered (900 w.) microwave. If yours has less power, you may need to lengthen the cooking time. For smooth-textured polenta, follow stirring directions carefully.

5-6 Servings

Beans and Meat

- ¾ lb. ground round of beef
- 1 large onion, finely chopped
- 2 large garlic cloves, minced
- 1 14½-oz. can diced tomatoes, including juice
- 1 15-oz. can tomato sauce
- 4 cups cooked kidney beans *or* 2 15-oz. cans kidney beans, well drained
- 1½ tablespoons chili powder, or to taste
- ⅛ teaspoon ground black pepper
  Salt to taste (optional)

Polenta

- 1⅓ cups yellow cornmeal
- 1 tablespoon sugar
- ¾ teaspoon salt, or to taste (optional)
- 3 cups water

1 cup 1% fat milk
1 medium onion, diced
1 tablespoon canned chopped green chilies

Beans and Meat: In large, heavy pot, combine ground round, onion, and garlic. Cook over medium heat until browned, stirring frequently and breaking up meat with spoon. Turn out mixture onto plate lined with paper towels. When fat has been absorbed, return mixture to pot.

Add tomatoes, tomato sauce, kidney beans, chili powder, and pepper. Stir to mix well. Add salt to taste, if desired. Bring to a boil. Reduce heat, cover, and simmer 45 minutes, stirring occasionally, until flavors are well blended. Skim off and discard any fat.

Polenta: While sauce is cooking, combine cornmeal, sugar, salt, if desired, water, milk, onion, and green chilies in 2½-qt. microwave-safe casserole. Stir to mix well. Microwave, uncovered, on high power 8 to 9 minutes, stopping and stirring with wire whisk after 3 minutes and 6 minutes. After cooking, stir again with wire whisk until mixture is smooth. Cover with casserole lid and microwave an additional 6 to 7 minutes on high power. Remove from microwave and let stand an additional 3 to 4 minutes.

Serve meat and bean mixture over polenta.

Nutritional Data (based on 6 servings)

PER SERVING		EXCHANGES	
Calories	397	Milk	0.0
Fat (gm)	4.5	Veg.	3.0
Sat. Fat (gm)	1.2	Fruit	0.0
Cholesterol (mg)	29	Bread	3.0
Sodium (mg)	740	Meat	2.0
Protein (gm)	26.6	Fat	0.0
Carbohydrate (gm)	65.9		
% Calories from fat	10		

TEX-MEX DINNER

Through the magic of microwave cooking, you can have this spicy dish on the table in record time. Note that the recipe was developed using a high-powered microwave (900 w.). If yours has less power, you may need to microwave the casserole a bit longer.

5-7 Servings

¾ lb. ground round of beef
1 large onion, finely chopped
1 large green bell pepper, seeded and chopped
1 garlic clove, minced
1 14½-oz. can reduced-sodium diced tomatoes *or* regular diced tomatoes, including juice
1 16-oz. can reduced-sodium kidney beans *or* regular kidney beans, well drained
2 cups cooked garbanzo beans or 1 15-oz. can garbanzo beans, well drained
1 15-oz. can tomato sauce
1 tablespoon chili powder
1 teaspoon ground cumin
¼ teaspoon black pepper
¼ teaspoon salt, or to taste (optional)
Dash cayenne pepper (optional)
1 cup instant rice

In 3-qt. microwave-safe casserole, stir together ground round, onion, green pepper, and garlic. Cover and microwave on high power 5 to 7 minutes or until meat is cooked through, turning casserole one-quarter turn, stirring meat, and breaking it up one or two times during microwaving. With large spoon, break up any remaining large pieces of meat.

Turn out meat mixture onto large plate lined with paper towels to absorb any excess fat. Return to casserole.

Add tomatoes, kidney beans, garbanzo beans, tomato sauce, chili powder, cumin, black pepper, salt, if desired, and cayenne pepper, if desired.

Cover with casserole lid and microwave on high power 12 to 15 minutes or until flavors are well blended, turning casserole one-quarter turn and stirring once or twice during microwaving. Stir in rice. Re-cover and microwave an additional 6 to 8 minutes or until rice is tender, stirring once or twice during microwaving.

Nutritional Data (based on 7 servings)

PER SERVING		EXCHANGES	
Calories	286	Milk	0.0
Fat (gm)	3.7	Veg.	3.0
Sat. Fat (gm)	0.7	Fruit	0.0
Cholesterol (mg)	23.4	Bread	2.0
Sodium (mg)	414	Meat	1.0
Protein (gm)	19.8	Fat	0.0
Carbohydrate (gm)	45.3		
% Calories from fat	11		

PITA POCKETS

◆

These hearty, hot sandwiches certainly qualify as a meal in themselves. And the microwave makes preparation a snap.

7-9 Servings

Filling

- ¾ lb. ground round of beef
- 1 large onion, chopped
- 2 garlic cloves, minced
- 2 cups chopped cauliflower florets
- 1 red bell pepper, seeded and diced
- 2½ cups cooked cannellini beans *or* 1 19-oz. can cannellini beans, well drained
- ½ cup dark raisins
- ½ cup ketchup
- 1 tablespoon apple cider vinegar
- 2 teaspoons dried thyme leaves
- 1½ teaspoons dried marjoram leaves
- ½ teaspoon ground cinnamon
  Dash ground cloves
- ¾ teaspoon salt, or to taste (optional)
- ¼ teaspoon black pepper

To Serve

- 7-9 medium pitas, cut in half to make 2 pockets each

Filling: In 3-qt. microwave-safe casserole, stir together ground round, onion, garlic, cauliflower, and red pepper. Cover with casserole lid, and microwave on high power 8 to 10 minutes until meat is cooked through, turning casserole one-quarter turn, stirring meat, and breaking it up twice during microwaving. With large spoon, break up any remaining large pieces of meat.

Turn out meat mixture onto large plate lined with paper towels to absorb any excess fat. Return to casserole.

Add beans, raisins, ketchup, vinegar, thyme, marjoram, cinnamon, cloves, salt, if using, and black pepper. Cover with casserole lid, and microwave on high power 4 to 5 minutes or until heated through, turning casserole one-quarter turn and stirring contents once during microwaving.

To Serve: Gently spoon mixture into pita pockets, being careful not to overfill them.

Nutritional Data (based on 9 servings)

PER SERVING		EXCHANGES	
Calories	318	Milk	0.0
Fat (gm)	9.7	Veg.	2.5
Sat. Fat (gm)	3.2	Fruit	0.5
Cholesterol (mg)	27	Bread	1.5
Sodium (mg)	488	Meat	1.0
Protein (gm)	16	Fat	1.5
Carbohydrate (gm)	43		
% Calories from fat	27		

PIZZA WITH THE WORKS

In this case, pizza includes vegetables as well as meat for a hearty "one-dish meal." The vegetables and meat are cooked together in a skillet before they're added to the pizza.

4 Servings

- 6 ozs. ground round of beef
- 1 medium onion, chopped
- 1 large garlic clove, diced
- ¾ cup diced zucchini
- ½ red bell pepper, seeded and diced
- ½ teaspoon Italian seasoning
- ¼ teaspoon salt (optional)
- ⅛ teaspoon black pepper
- ⅔ cup reduced-fat pizza sauce
- 1 large unbaked Neapolitan-style (thin crust) pizza shell
- 3 ozs. (1 cup loosely packed) shredded reduced-fat mozzarella
- 4 large black or green olives with pimiento, sliced (optional)

Preheat oven to 450° F.

In large, non-stick skillet, combine ground round, onion, garlic, zucchini, red pepper, Italian seasoning, salt, if desired, and black pepper. Cook over medium heat, stirring frequently, until meat has browned and onion is tender, about 7 to 8 minutes. Remove skillet from heat. Turn out meat mixture onto large plate lined with paper towels to absorb excess fat and liquid. Return mixture to pan.

Meanwhile, spread pizza sauce evenly over pizza shell, leaving a ¼-inch ring of crust at outer edge. Sprinkle evenly with cheese. Spread meat and vegetable mixture evenly over all. Sprinkle on olives, if desired. Bake 7 to 9 minutes, or according to package directions, until edges of crust are browned. Cut into 8 wedges.

Nutritional Data

PER SERVING		EXCHANGES	
Calories	407	Milk	0.0
Fat (gm)	9.2	Veg.	2.0
Sat. Fat (gm)	2.0	Fruit	0.0
Cholesterol (mg)	35	Bread	3.0
Sodium (mg)	379	Meat	2.0
Protein (gm)	25	Fat	0.5
Carbohydrate (gm)	58		
% Calories from fat	20		

BEEF AND SOUR CREAM POTATO TOPPER

Sour cream and beef are both a natural with baked potatoes—which is why I combined them in this tasty entrée.

4-5 Servings

¾ lb. ground round of beef
1 large onion, chopped
1 large garlic clove, minced
1 large green bell pepper, seeded and chopped
1 large carrot, peeled and very thinly sliced
1 cup beef bouillon
2 tablespoons tomato paste
1½ teaspoons Dijon-style mustard
1 teaspoon dried thyme leaves
1 teaspoon dried marjoram leaves
½ teaspoon salt, or to taste (optional)
¼ teaspoon black pepper
2-3 drops hot pepper sauce (optional)
¾ cup non-fat sour cream
4-5 large baked potatoes

In large skillet, combine beef, onion, garlic, green pepper, and carrot. Cook over medium heat, stirring frequently, until beef is browned and onion is soft, about 7 or 8 minutes. Remove skillet from burner. Turn meat mixture out onto plate covered with paper towels to absorb any excess fat. Return mixture to skillet, and return to burner.

Add bouillon and tomato paste, stirring to combine well. Stir in mustard, thyme, marjoram, salt, if desired, black pepper, and hot pepper sauce, if desired. Simmer, covered, 10 to 12 minutes.

Stir in sour cream and cook 1 or 2 minutes longer. Serve over baked potatoes.

Nutritional Data (based on 5 servings)

PER SERVING		EXCHANGES	
Calories	314	Milk	0.0
Fat (gm)	8.7	Veg.	1.5
Sat. Fat (gm)	3.4	Fruit	0.0
Cholesterol (mg)	42	Bread	2.0
Sodium (mg)	253	Meat	2.0
Protein (gm)	19	Fat	0.5
Carbohydrate (gm)	40		
% Calories from fat	25		

TEXAS POTATOES

*With this spicy topping and your microwave, it's a snap
to turn baked potatoes into a meal.*

5-6 Servings

¾ lb. ground round of beef
1 large onion, chopped
1 garlic clove, minced
1 14½-oz. can tomatoes, including juice
1 8-oz. can tomato sauce
1 16-oz. can reduced-sodium kidney beans *or*
  regular kidney beans, well drained
2 tablespoons canned chopped green chilies
1 tablespoon granulated sugar
2 teaspoons chili powder
¼ teaspoon black pepper
4-6 baked potatoes

In 3-qt. microwave-safe casserole, stir together ground round, onion, and garlic. Cover with casserole lid, and microwave on high power 7 to 9 minutes or until meat is cooked through, turning casserole one-quarter turn, stirring meat, and breaking it up twice during microwaving. With large spoon, break up any remaining large pieces of meat.

Turn out meat mixture onto large plate lined with paper towels to absorb any excess fat. Return mixture to casserole.

Add tomatoes, tomato sauce, beans, chilies, sugar, chili powder, and black pepper. Cover with casserole lid, and microwave on high power 4 to 5 minutes or until heated through, turning casserole one-quarter turn and stirring contents once during microwaving.

Serve topping over baked potatoes.

Nutritional Data (based on 6 servings)

PER SERVING		EXCHANGES	
Calories	323	Milk	0.0
Fat (gm)	2.7	Veg.	2.0
Sat. Fat (gm)	0.7	Fruit	0.0
Cholesterol (mg)	27.4	Bread	3.0
Sodium (mg)	404	Meat	1.0
Protein (gm)	19.5	Fat	0.0
Carbohydrate (gm)	57.4		
% Calories from fat	7		

AUSTRIAN PORK LOIN WITH APPLES AND CRANBERRY SAUCE

---

*This is a delicious and unusual recipe that features a
tangy medley of lean pork, fruit, and spices.*

4-5 Servings

Pork and Fruit

- 1 lb. boneless pork loin, trimmed of all fat and cut into ¼-inch slices
- ½ teaspoon dried thyme leaves
- ¼ teaspoon black pepper
- ¼ teaspoon salt (optional)
- 1 cup chopped onion
- 2 teaspoons non-diet, tub-style margarine or butter
- 2 large, tart apples, peeled, cored, and thinly sliced
- 1 16-oz. can whole cranberry sauce
- 1 tablespoon Worcestershire sauce
- 1 tablespoon apple cider vinegar
- 2 tablespoons, packed, brown sugar

To Serve

- 8-10 ozs. reduced-fat egg noodles, cooked according to package directions

Pork and Fruit:

Sprinkle pork with thyme, pepper, and salt, if desired. In Dutch oven or similar large, heavy pot, combine pork, onion, and margarine. Cook over medium heat, stirring frequently, until pork has changed color.

Add apples, cranberry sauce, Worcestershire sauce, vinegar, and brown sugar and stir to mix well. Bring to a boil. Reduce heat, cover, and simmer 40 minutes, stirring occasionally, until pork is tender.

Serve over cooked noodles.

Nutritional Data (based on 5 servings)

PER SERVING		EXCHANGES	
Calories	460	Milk	0.0
Fat (gm)	8.5	Veg.	0.0
Sat. Fat (gm)	2.4	Fruit	3.0
Cholesterol (mg)	77	Bread	2.0
Sodium (mg)	123	Meat	2.0
Protein (gm)	19	Fat	0.5
Carbohydrate (gm)	79		
% Calories from fat	17		

PORK LOIN AND SAUERKRAUT

————————◆————————

*Since sauerkraut is a bit high in sodium, I use no more than
I need for flavor and reserve it for special dishes. Here's
one—a wonderful combination of pork and sauerkraut,
flavored with caraway. Microwaving the potatoes
and onions speeds preparation.*

4-5 Servings

1 lb. lean pork loin, thinly sliced and cut into
  bite-sized pieces
2 teaspoons olive oil
1 lb. potatoes, peeled and cut into thin slices (3½
  cups)
1 large onion, finely chopped
1 16-oz. can reduced-sodium tomatoes *or* regular
  tomatoes
1 teaspoon caraway seeds
¼ teaspoon black pepper
1 16-oz. package fresh sauerkraut, well drained
¼ cup non-fat sour cream

Combine pork and oil in large, non-stick skillet. Saute pork over medium
heat until it changes color. Remove skillet from burner.

Meanwhile combine potatoes and onion in 4-cup measure or similar small
microwave-safe bowl. Cover with wax paper, and microwave on high power
7 to 8 minutes or until potatoes are almost tender, stopping to stir once
and turn container one-quarter turn.

Return skillet with pork to burner. Add tomatoes, breaking them up with spoon. Stir in caraway and pepper. Stir in potatoes and onion, then sauerkraut. Bring to a boil, reduce heat, and simmer 25 minutes.

Remove skillet from burner. Stir in sour cream. Return to burner and cook on very low heat 2 or 3 minutes longer or until sauce is heated through.

Nutritional Data (based on 5 servings)

PER SERVING		EXCHANGES	
Calories	245	Milk	0.0
Fat (gm)	7	Veg.	2.0
Sat. Fat (gm)	2	Fruit	0.0
Cholesterol (mg)	39.7	Bread	1.0
Sodium (mg)	650	Meat	2.0
Protein (gm)	18.2	Fat	0.0
Carbohydrate (gm)	28.5		
% Calories from fat	25		

PORK STIR-FRY

◆

Quick-cooking noodles called rice sticks help make this a super-fast meal. They and the Hoisin sauce are available at specialty markets and some grocery stores.

5 Servings

1 lb. pork loin slices, trimmed of all fat and cut into thin strips
1 large onion, finely chopped
1 large garlic clove, minced
⅔ cup defatted chicken broth, divided
2 teaspoons sesame oil
2 tablespoons reduced-sodium soy sauce
1 tablespoon Hoisin sauce
2 teaspoons rice vinegar *or* white vinegar
2-3 drops hot oil (optional)
4 cups sliced bok choy leaves and stems
½ red bell pepper, seeded and diced
3½ ozs. rice sticks, cooked according to package directions

In a large, non-stick, spray-coated skillet, cook pork over medium heat until white on both sides. Remove and reserve in medium bowl.

Add onion, garlic, 3 tablespoons broth, and oil to skillet. Cook over medium heat, stirring frequently, 7 to 8 minutes or until onion is tender. Add soy sauce, Hoisin sauce, vinegar, hot oil, if desired, and remaining broth. Return pork to pan.

Cover and simmer 15 to 20 minutes or until pork is cooked through. Add bok choy and red pepper and cook, uncovered, an additional 5 or 6 minutes.

Stir rice sticks into skillet.

Nutritional Data

PER SERVING		EXCHANGES	
Calories	238	Milk	0.0
Fat (gm)	5.6	Veg.	1.0
Sat. Fat (gm)	1.4	Fruit	0.0
Cholesterol (mg)	65	Bread	1.0
Sodium (mg)	359	Meat	2.5
Protein (gm)	23	Fat	0.0
Carbohydrate (gm)	23		
% Calories from fat	21		

FINNISH PORK WITH BEETS

◆

When I first encountered this Scandinavian recipe in a vintage cookbook, I wondered how it would taste. But since I love beets, I decided to update it and give it a try. Not only is it tasty—it's also colorful.

4-5 Servings

Pork and Vegetables

   1 lb. boneless pork loin, sliced into narrow 2-inch strips
  ½ teaspoon salt (optional)
  ¼ teaspoon black pepper
   1 cup chopped onion
   1 16-oz. can sliced beets
   3 tablespoons apple cider vinegar
  ½ cup defatted beef broth
 1½ teaspoons prepared horseradish
  ½ teaspoon dried thyme leaves
   2 teaspoons cornstarch
  ¼ cup cold water

Salt to taste (optional)
Pepper to taste (optional)

To Serve

8-9 ozs. reduced-fat egg noodles, cooked according to package directions

Pork and Vegetables:

Sprinkle pork with salt, if desired, and pepper. In large, non-stick spray-
coated skillet, cook pork and onion over medium heat, stirring frequently,
until pork has changed color.

Drain beets in sieve, reserving juice. Cut beets into shoestring strips and
reserve. Combine ½ cup beet juice with vinegar. Add to pan along with
broth, horseradish, and thyme. Bring to a boil. Cover, reduce heat, and
simmer 20 minutes.

Combine cornstarch and water. Add to skillet and stir to mix well. Cook
until sauce thickens slightly. Add beets. Re-cover and cook an additional 5
minutes. Add salt and pepper to taste, if desired.

Serve pork and beet mixture over cooked egg noodles.

Nutritional Data (based on 5 servings)

PER SERVING		EXCHANGES	
Calories	291	Milk	0.0
Fat (gm)	6.9	Veg.	1.5
Sat. Fat (gm)	2.2	Fruit	0.0
Cholesterol (mg)	78	Bread	2.0
Sodium (mg)	345	Meat	2.0
Protein (gm)	20	Fat	0.0
Carbohydrate (gm)	38		
% Calories from fat	21		

POLENTA WITH HAM AND PEPPERS

Polenta, cooked yellow cornmeal, can be used in place of pasta with a variety of sauces. This microwave method not only speeds cooking but also helps eliminate lumps and the almost constant stirring necessary when polenta is made on top of the stove. The recipe was created with a high-powered microwave (900 w.). If yours has less power, you may need to lengthen the cooking time.

5-6 Servings

Polenta

- 1⅓ cups yellow cornmeal
- 1 tablespoon granulated sugar
- ½ teaspoon salt, or to taste (optional)
- 3 cups water
- 1 cup 1% fat milk

Ham and Vegetables

- 1 medium onion, chopped
- 1 garlic clove, minced
- 2 teaspoons olive oil
- 1 14½-oz. can reduced-sodium diced tomatoes, including juice *or* regular diced tomatoes
- 1 15-oz. can reduced-sodium tomato sauce *or* regular tomato sauce
- ½ lb. reduced-sodium, fully cooked ham steak, cut into bite-sized pieces
- 1½ cups mixed frozen green, red, and yellow bell peppers
- 1 bay leaf
- 1½ teaspoons Italian seasoning
- ¼ teaspoon black pepper

To Serve

- 2 teaspoons grated Parmesan cheese per serving for garnish (optional)

Polenta: Combine cornmeal, sugar, salt, if desired, water and milk in 3-qt. microwave-safe casserole. Stir to mix well. Microwave, uncovered, on high power 8 to 9 minutes, stopping and stirring with wire whisk after 3 and 6 minutes. After cooking, stir again with wire whisk until mixture is smooth. Cover with casserole lid and microwave an additional 6 to 7 minutes on high power. Remove from microwave and let stand an additional 3 to 4 minutes.

Ham and Vegetables: Meanwhile, in large, non-stick skillet, combine onion, garlic, and olive oil. Cook over medium heat, stirring frequently, until onion begins to soften, about 4 to 5 minutes.

Add tomatoes, tomato sauce, ham, peppers, bay leaf, Italian seasoning, and pepper. Stir to mix well. Bring to a boil. Simmer, uncovered, until vegetables are tender and sauce has thickened somewhat, about 15 minutes. Remove bay leaf.

To Serve: Spoon a portion of polenta onto each plate. Top with ham-vegetable mixture. Garnish with Parmesan cheese, if desired.

Nutritional Data (based on 6 servings)

PER SERVING		EXCHANGES	
Calories	247	Milk	0.0
Fat (gm)	4.8	Veg.	3.0
Sat. Fat (gm)	0.6	Fruit	0.0
Cholesterol (mg)	1.7	Bread	2.0
Sodium (mg)	261	Meat	0.0
Protein (gm)	9.1	Fat	0.5
Carbohydrate (gm)	44.1		
% Calories from fat	17		

SCALLOPED HAM AND POTATOES

This ham, cheese, and potatoes bake is considerably reduced in fat from the traditional version, yet it makes a wonderfully satisfying home-style meal. The microwave speeds preparation.

5-6 Servings

- 6 cups thinly sliced new red potatoes, peeled (about 1¾ lbs.)
- 1 large onion, chopped
- 1 small garlic clove, minced
- 2 tablespoons cornstarch
- 1¾ cups 1% fat milk
- ½ teaspoon dried thyme leaves
- ½ teaspoon dried basil leaves
- ¼ teaspoon dry mustard
- ⅛ teaspoon white pepper
- ⅛ teaspoon salt, or to taste (optional)
- 3 ozs. grated reduced-fat sharp Cheddar cheese (¾ cup)
- 8 ozs. reduced-sodium ham steak, trimmed of all fat and cut into bite-sized pieces

Preheat oven to 350° F.

Combine potatoes, onion, and garlic in non-stick, spray-coated, oven-proof, microwave-safe 2½-qt. casserole. Stir to mix well. Cover with wax paper and microwave on high power, stirring twice and turning casserole one-quarter turn, 7 to 9 minutes or until potatoes are partially cooked.

Meanwhile, place cornstarch in medium saucepan. Gradually add milk, stirring to make sure mixture remains smooth. Add thyme, basil, mustard, pepper, and salt, if desired. Stir to mix. Bring to simmer over medium heat, stirring frequently. Reduce heat and cook, stirring, until milk has thickened. Reduce heat to low. Cook 1 minute longer, stirring. Stir in cheese and continue to stir until melted.

Add ham to casserole with potatoes and onions, and stir to mix well. Pour sauce over all, and stir to mix well. Bake in 350° F. oven, covered, 30 to 40 minutes or until potatoes are tender, stirring once. (Make sure bay leaf is visible after stirring.) For a crusty top, remove cover during last 20 minutes of baking. Remove bay leaf and discard.

Allow casserole to sit about 5 minutes before serving.

Nutritional Data (based on 6 servings)

PER SERVING		EXCHANGES	
Calories	386	Milk	0.5
Fat (gm)	6.5	Veg.	0.0
Sat. Fat (gm)	3	Fruit	0.0
Cholesterol (mg)	32	Bread	3.5
Sodium (mg)	601	Meat	2.0
Protein (gm)	19	Fat	0.0
Carbohydrate (gm)	64		
% Calories from fat	15		

TANGY BEANS AND BACON OVER PASTA

Because Canadian bacon comes from the pork loin, it's low in fat. Happily, it's also very flavorful, so a little bit can add a wonderful smoked-meat taste to recipes such as this hearty dish, which is served Italian-style, over pasta.

6-7 Servings

Beans and Bacon

1 large onion, finely chopped

1 large clove garlic, minced

2 teaspoons olive oil

¾ cup defatted beef broth *or* bouillon, divided

1 15-oz. can tomato sauce

2½ cups cooked Great Northern beans or 1 19-oz. can white kidney beans, well drained

½ large green bell pepper, seeded and diced

½ large red bell pepper, seeded and diced (if unavailable, substitute green pepper)

1 teaspoon dried thyme leaves

½ teaspoon dried basil leaves

¼ teaspoon dry mustard

1 bay leaf

¼ teaspoon black pepper, or to taste

6 ozs. Canadian bacon, trimmed of all fat and cut into narrow strips

¼ cup non-fat ricotta cheese

Pasta

1½ cups medium-sized pasta, such as cut fusilli

Beans and Bacon: In Dutch oven or other large, heavy pot, combine onion and garlic with oil and 2 tablespoons broth. Cook, stirring, over medium heat, about 5 or 6 minutes or until onion is tender. If liquid begins to evaporate, add a bit more broth.

Add tomato sauce, remaining broth, beans, green pepper, red pepper, thyme, basil, mustard, bay leaf, and black pepper. Stir to mix well. Bring to a boil. Reduce heat, cover, and simmer 10 minutes.

Add bacon and simmer an additional 15 minutes or until flavors are well blended. Remove bean mixture from heat. Remove bay leaf and discard. Stir in ricotta.

Pasta: Cook according to package directions. Serve individual portions of bean and bacon mixture over pasta.

Nutritional Data (based on 7 servings)

PER SERVING		EXCHANGES	
Calories	255	Milk	0.0
Fat (gm)	4.3	Veg.	1.0
Sat. Fat (gm)	1.0	Fruit	0.0
Cholesterol (mg)	15	Bread	2.0
Sodium (mg)	787	Meat	1.5
Protein (gm)	17	Fat	0.0
Carbohydrate (gm)	39		
% Calories from fat	15		

BACON, BEAN, AND POTATO DINNER

Here's an interesting combination—Canadian bacon, potatoes, and kidney beans blended together in a home-style casserole with a Southwestern flavor.

5-6 Servings

2   teaspoons non-diet, tub-style margarine
    or butter
1   cup chopped onion
1   garlic clove, minced
2   tablespoons white flour
½   teaspoon chili powder
1   cup (generous) 1% fat milk
6   ozs. Canadian bacon, cut into narrow strips
1   16-oz. can reduced-sodium *or* regular kidney
    beans, drained
½   cup mild or medium picante sauce
¼   teaspoon black pepper
¼   teaspoon salt, or to taste (optional)
3   cups thinly sliced, peeled potatoes

Preheat oven to 350° F.

In oven-proof, flame-proof, 2½-qt. casserole, combine margarine, onion, and garlic. Cook over medium heat, stirring frequently, until onion is tender, 5 or 6 minutes. Stir in flour and chili powder until well combined.

Gradually stir in milk, being careful to keep mixture smooth. Continue to cook, stirring, until mixture thickens. Remove casserole from burner. Stir in bacon, beans, picante sauce, pepper, and salt, if using. Stir in potatoes.

Cover and bake 1 hour, stirring after 30 minutes, or until potato slices are almost tender. Remove cover and bake an additional 10 to 15 minutes until potato slices begin to brown on top.

Nutritional Data (based on 6 servings)

PER SERVING		EXCHANGES	
Calories	267	Milk	0.0
Fat (gm)	4.5	Veg.	1.0
Sat. Fat (gm)	1.2	Fruit	0.0
Cholesterol (mg)	15.2	Bread	2.5
Sodium (mg)	553	Meat	1.0
Protein (gm)	14.3	Fat	0.0
Carbohydrate (gm)	43.9		
% Calories from fat	15		

PASTA VASULE

You may have heard of this thick, flavorful Italian soup, even if you weren't sure of the ingredients. Traditionally, it's made with one of the simplest pasta shapes—elbow macaroni. The name is pronounced "pasta vazooooolee"—with a lip-smacking sound.

5-6 Servings

- 2 teaspoons olive oil
- 1 large onion, chopped
- 1 large garlic clove, minced
- 3½ cups reduced-sodium defatted beef broth *or* regular defatted beef broth, divided
- 1 large carrot, peeled and finely chopped
- 1 large celery stalk, finely chopped
- 1 14¼-oz. can Italian-style tomatoes, including juice, chopped
- 2½ cups cooked white kidney beans *or* 1 19-oz. can white kidney beans, drained
- 8 ozs. ham steak, trimmed of all fat and cut into bite-sized pieces
- ½ teaspoon dried oregano leaves
- ½ teaspoon dried basil leaves
- ⅛ teaspoon black pepper
- 3 ozs. uncooked small elbow pasta or other medium-size pasta (2 cups cooked pasta)

To Serve

- 1 tablespoon grated Parmesan cheese per serving

In large, heavy pot, combine oil, onion, garlic, and 3 tablespoons broth. Cook over medium heat 5 or 6 minutes or until onion is soft. If liquid begins to evaporate, add more broth.

Add remaining broth along with carrot, celery, tomatoes, beans, ham, oregano, basil, and pepper. Cover and simmer 35 to 40 minutes, stirring occasionally, until vegetables are tender and flavors are well blended.

Meanwhile, cook pasta according to package directions and drain well in colander. Add pasta to mixture, and simmer an additional 2 or 3 minutes.

Serve in soup bowls, and sprinkle individual portions with Parmesan cheese.

Nutritional Data (based on 6 servings)

PER SERVING		EXCHANGES	
Calories	287	Milk	0.0
Fat (gm)	6.7	Veg.	1.0
Sat. Fat (gm)	2.2	Fruit	0.0
Cholesterol (mg)	37	Bread	2.0
Sodium (mg)	716	Meat	2.0
Protein (gm)	21	Fat	0.5
Carbohydrate (gm)	36		
% Calories from fat	21		

SWEET-AND-SOUR CABBAGE SOUP

Here's a rich, tangy soup that evokes the flavor of stuffed cabbage, but it's much quicker and easier to make. Combining ground beef and ground turkey breast in the recipe significantly reduces the fat content. Be sure to use ground turkey breast as it is much lower in fat than regular ground turkey.

8 Servings

- 8 ozs. ground round of beef
- 6 ozs. ground turkey breast
- 1 large onion, chopped
- 2 garlic cloves, minced
- 8 cups defatted reduced-sodium beef broth *or* regular defatted beef broth
- 1 15-oz. can tomato sauce
- 2 tablespoons apple cider vinegar
- 2 tablespoons packed brown sugar
- 1 large bay leaf
- 1 teaspoon dried thyme leaves
- ⅛ teaspoon ground cinnamon
  Dash ground cloves
- ¼ teaspoon black pepper
- 4 cups thinly sliced green cabbage
- 6 baby carrots, coarsely sliced
- ⅓ cup dark, *or* light, raisins
- ½ cup uncooked white rice
- ⅛ teaspoon salt or to taste (optional)

In a large, heavy Dutch oven or similar pot, combine beef, turkey, onion, and garlic. Cook over medium heat, stirring and breaking up meat, until beef is browned. If meat sticks, add a bit of broth.

Add broth, tomato sauce, vinegar, sugar, bay leaf, thyme, cinnamon, cloves, and pepper. Stir to mix well. Stir in cabbage, carrots, and raisins. Bring to a boil. Reduce heat, cover, and simmer 20 minutes. Add rice. Bring to a boil. Cover and boil 5 minutes. Reduce heat and simmer 25 to 30 minutes.

Remove and discard bay leaf. With a large, shallow spoon, skim any fat from top of soup and discard. Add salt, if desired.

Nutritional Data (based on 8 servings)

PER SERVING		EXCHANGES	
Calories	202	Milk	0.0
Fat (gm)	4.2	Veg.	1.0
Sat. Fat (gm)	1.7	Fruit	0.0
Cholesterol (mg)	25.8	Bread	1.0
Sodium (mg)	425	Meat	2.0
Protein (gm)	16.1	Fat	0.0
Carbohydrate (gm)	26.2		
% Calories from fat	18		

HEARTY BEAN AND BARLEY SOUP

◆

Bean and barley soup is one of my fondest childhood memories. However, my mother only made this delicious meal when we had a leftover ham bone. When I grew up, I discovered that the soup could also be made with smoked pork hocks. The hocks don't produce quite as rich a flavor, so I usually increase the number of bouillon cubes if I use them.

9 Servings

- 2 cups dry Great Northern beans, picked over and rinsed
- 9 cups water
- 1 meaty ham bone from reduced-sodium ham *or* 2 pork hocks (about 1½ lbs. total)
- ¼ cup pearl barley
- 2 cups chopped onion
- 2 large carrots, peeled and sliced
- 2 large celery stalks, including leaves, sliced
- 3 beef bouillon cubes (or up to 5, if needed)
- 2 garlic cloves, minced
- 3 bay leaves
- 1½ teaspoons dried thyme leaves
- ¼ teaspoon ground celery seed
- ¼ teaspoon black pepper
- 3 cups thinly sliced cabbage
- 1 8-oz. can reduced-sodium tomato sauce *or* regular tomato sauce
- Salt to taste (optional)

Place beans in large Dutch oven or soup pot. Cover with 2 inches of water and bring to boil over high heat. Lower heat and boil 2 minutes longer. Remove pot from heat, cover, and let beans stand 1 hour. Drain beans in colander, discarding water.

Return beans to pot in which they were cooked. Add water, ham bone, barley, onion, carrots, celery, 3 beef bouillon cubes, garlic, bay leaves, thyme leaves, celery seed, and pepper. Bring to boil, cover, lower heat, and simmer 1 hour, stirring occasionally.

Add cabbage and simmer an additional 30 to 40 minutes, stirring occasionally, until beans are very tender. Taste soup. If broth seems weak, add additional bouillon cube or cubes, and simmer an additional 10 minutes.

Turn off heat under soup pot. If ham bone has been used, remove and reserve. If pork hocks have been used, remove and discard. Remove and discard bay leaves. With large, shallow spoon, skim any fat from top of soup and discard.

When ham bone is cool enough to handle, cut lean meat into small pieces and return to soup. Add tomato sauce. Add salt, if desired, Stir well. Bring soup to a boil again. Reduce heat and simmer an additional 10 minutes.

Nutritional Data

PER SERVING		EXCHANGES	
Calories	180	Milk	0.0
Fat (gm)	1.7	Veg.	5.0
Sat. Fat (gm)	2.3	Fruit	0.0
Cholesterol (mg)	8	Bread	0.5
Sodium (mg)	523	Meat	0.5
Protein (gm)	12	Fat	0.0
Carbohydrate (gm)	31		
% Calories from fat	8		

POTATO, CORN, AND BACON CHOWDER

Here's one of my favorite soups, a delicious corn chowder enriched with the flavor of Canadian bacon. The pureed corn and potatoes add significantly to the creamy taste and texture. A blender purees easily and quickly and produces a very smooth-textured soup. You could also use a food processor, although the texture won't be quite as velvety.

5-6 Servings

- 2 teaspoons olive oil
- 1 large onion, chopped
- 1 garlic clove, minced
- 3½ cups defatted chicken broth, divided
- 2½ cups 1% fat milk
- 3½ cups peeled and cubed (½ in.) boiling potatoes
- 1 large bay leaf
- ¼ teaspoon powdered mustard
- ¾ teaspoon dried thyme leaves
- ¼ teaspoon white pepper
- 2½ cups frozen yellow corn kernels
- 6 ozs. Canadian bacon, cut into slivers
- ¼ teaspoon salt, or to taste (optional)

In a large pot, combine oil, onion, garlic, and 2 tablespoons broth. Cook over medium heat, stirring frequently, about 5 minutes or until onion is tender. If liquid begins to evaporate, add more broth. Add remaining broth, milk, potatoes, bay leaf, mustard, thyme, and pepper. Bring to a boil. Lower heat and simmer, covered, 10 to 11 minutes, stirring occasionally, until potatoes are tender. Add corn and bring liquid to a simmer again; simmer an additional 6 to 8 minutes until corn is cooked through.

Remove and discard bay leaf. Cool 5 minutes. Using ladle, transfer about half of vegetables and liquid, in batches if necessary, to blender container. Blend on medium speed until thoroughly pureed. Return puree to pot. Stir in Canadian bacon. Simmer 6 to 7 minutes longer. Add salt, if desired.

Nutritional Data (based on 6 servings)

PER SERVING		EXCHANGES	
Calories	306	Milk	0.5
Fat (gm)	5.9	Veg.	1.0
Sat. Fat (gm)	2.4	Fruit	0.0
Cholesterol (mg)	27	Bread	3.0
Sodium (mg)	873	Meat	1.0
Protein (gm)	16	Fat	0.5
Carbohydrate (gm)	50		
% Calories from fat	17		

LAMB BIRIANI

Biriani is a traditional Indian meat and rice dish that can be made with lamb, chicken, or beef. Although the meat can be served over long-grain white rice, it's worth using basmati rice, which can be bought at specialty markets.

4-5 Servings

Meat

- 1 lb. lamb leg cubes, trimmed of all fat
- 2 teaspoons tub-style margarine *or* butter
- 2 cups chopped onion
- 1 garlic clove, minced
- 1 cup defatted chicken broth, divided
- 1 teaspoon ground coriander
- 1 teaspoon ground ginger
- ½ teaspoon chili powder
- ¼ teaspoon ground cinnamon
- ¼ teaspoon ground cloves
- ¾ cup non-fat plain yogurt

Rice

- 2 teaspoons tub-style margarine *or* butter
- 2¼ cups defatted chicken broth, divided
- 1 cup chopped onion
- 1 cup uncooked basmati *or* other long-grain rice
  Pinch of saffron, soaked in 2 tablespoons hot water for 10 minutes
- ¼ teaspoon white pepper
- 1 medium carrot, peeled and grated or shredded

Garnish

Parsley sprigs (optional)

Meat: In spray-coated Dutch oven or similar pot, cook lamb cubes over medium heat until browned on all sides. Remove and set aside. In same pot, combine margarine, onion, garlic, and 3 tablespoons broth. Cook over medium heat, stirring frequently, 5 or 6 minutes or until onion is soft.

Stir in coriander, ginger, chili powder, cinnamon, and cloves into onion mixture. Stir in yogurt. Stir in remaining broth. Return meat to pot. Bring to boil. Cover, reduce heat, and simmer 30 minutes or until meat is tender, stirring occasionally.

Rice: In 2-qt. saucepan, combine margarine, 3 tablespoons broth, and onion. Cook, stirring frequently, until onion is soft, about 5 or 6 minutes. Add rice and continue cooking, stirring constantly, for 2 minutes. Add saffron, with its liquid, and pepper and stir. Add remaining broth and carrot and stir. Bring to boil. Cover, reduce heat, and simmer 15 to 20 minutes or until rice is tender.

Layer rice and meat mixture in casserole and serve. Alternatively, transfer rice to serving platter and serve meat over it.

Garnish with parsley sprigs, if desired.

Nutritional Data (based on 5 servings)

PER SERVING		EXCHANGES	
Calories	280	Milk	0.0
Fat (gm)	8.2	Veg.	1.5
Sat. Fat (gm)	2.1	Fruit	0.0
Cholesterol (mg)	46	Bread	1.5
Sodium (mg)	332	Meat	2.0
Protein (gm)	22	Fat	0.5
Carbohydrate (gm)	30		
% Calories from fat	26		

SAVORY LAMB SHANKS

◆

*Here's a rich and flavorful combination of lamb,
lentils, vegetables, and spices.*

6-7 Servings

2 lbs. lamb shanks
1 tablespoon white flour
2 cups chopped onion
2 garlic cloves, minced
2 teaspoons olive oil
2 cups defatted chicken broth, divided
1 14½-oz. can tomatoes, including juice
2 large carrots, peeled and sliced
½ cup brown lentils
1 medium green bell pepper, seeded and cubed
¼ cup chopped fresh parsley leaves
2 bay leaves
2 teaspoon dried thyme leaves
¼ teaspoon ground cinnamon
⅛ teaspoon ground cloves
⅛ teaspoon ground black pepper
1¼ cups uncooked brown rice
Parsley sprigs for garnish (optional)

Preheat broiler. Adjust rack about 3 inches from heating element.

In shallow baking pan, sprinkle flour over lamb shanks. Stir to coat with flour. Spread out pieces so they are separated from one another. Broil 10 to 14 minutes or until shanks are browned on all sides, turning once or twice. Remove from pan with slotted spoon.

Meanwhile, in Dutch oven or similar large, heavy pot, combine onion, garlic, oil, and 3 tablespoons broth. Cook over medium heat, stirring, 6 or 7 minutes or until onion is tender. If liquid begins to evaporate, add a bit more broth.

Add lamb shanks to pot, along with remaining broth, tomatoes, carrots, lentils, green pepper, parsley, bay leaves, thyme, cinnamon, cloves, and black pepper. Stir to mix well, breaking up tomatoes with spoon. Bring to a boil. Cover, reduce heat, and simmer 1½ to 2 hours or until lamb shanks are tender, stirring occasionally.

After lamb has cooked about 1 hour, cook brown rice according to package directions.

Remove and discard bay leaves from lamb mixture. Remove and reserve lamb shanks. Carefully skim off and discard any fat from surface of liquid. When shanks are cool enough to handle, cut off lean meat and return it to pot. Discard bones and fat.

Arrange rice on serving platter. Top with lamb mixture. Garnish with parsley sprigs, if desired.

Nutritional Data (based on 7 servings)

PER SERVING		EXCHANGES	
Calories	325	Milk	0.0
Fat (gm)	7.8	Veg.	1.5
Sat. Fat (gm)	2.2	Fruit	0.0
Cholesterol (mg)	56	Bread	2.0
Sodium (mg)	246	Meat	2.5
Protein (gm)	25	Fat	0.0
Carbohydrate (gm)	40		
% Calories from fat	22		

LAMB, SPLIT PEA, BEAN, AND BARLEY SOUP

◆

If you like split pea soup made with a ham bone, try this slightly milder variation, using lamb.

8-9 Servings

- 11 cups water
- 3 lbs. lamb shanks (3 shanks)
- 2 cups (1 lb.) dry green split peas, picked over and rinsed
- ¼ cup pearl barley
- ¾ cup dry navy or Great Northern beans, picked over and rinsed
- 3 large bay leaves
- 2 beef bouillon cubes (or up to 5, as needed)
- 2 large onions, coarsely chopped
- 2 large carrots, thinly sliced
- 2 large celery stalks, including leaves, thinly sliced
- 2 garlic cloves, minced
- 1½ teaspoons dried thyme leaves

    1 teaspoon dried basil leaves
    ½ teaspoon ground celery seed
  1-2 teaspoons salt, or to taste (optional)
    ½ teaspoon black pepper

In large, heavy soup pot, combine water, lamb shanks, split peas, barley, and beans. Bring to boil over high heat. Add bay leaves, 2 bouillon cubes, onion, carrots, celery, garlic, thyme, basil, and celery seed. Cover and lower heat. Simmer, stirring occasionally, until beans are tender and split peas have thickened soup, about 2 to 2½ hours.

As soup thickens, lower heat and stir more frequently to prevent split peas from sticking to bottom of pot. Remove bay leaves. Taste soup. If flavor seems weak, add more bouillon cubes. Add salt, if desired, and pepper.

When beans are tender, remove lamb shanks from pot. When cool enough to handle, cut off lean meat and return meat to pot. Carefully skim any fat from top of soup with large, shallow spoon; or refrigerate overnight and remove solid fat layer.

This soup is excellent reheated. However, it must be stirred carefully to prevent split peas from sticking to pot. If soup thickens too much in refrigerator, thin with a bit more water during reheating.

Nutritional Data (based on 9 servings)

PER SERVING		EXCHANGES	
Calories	331	Milk	0.0
Fat (gm)	4.1	Veg.	1.0
Sat. Fat (gm)	1.3	Fruit	0.0
Cholesterol (mg)	41	Bread	2.5
Sodium (mg)	253	Meat	2.5
Protein (gm)	29	Fat	0.0
Carbohydrate (gm)	46		
% Calories from fat	11		

3
POULTRY

A ll cuts of poultry are not created equal. While turkey and chicken breast are very low in fat (0.6 grams for a three-ounce portion of skinless turkey breast and 3 grams for the same amount of skinless chicken breast), dark meat is another story. Three ounces of turkey leg with skin have 8.3 grams while three ounces of chicken thigh with skin have over 13 grams—almost as much as sirloin steak.

So all of the recipes in this chapter—such as Arroz con Pollo, Artichoke "Stuffed" Turkey, and Caribbean-Style Chicken with Black Beans—are made with either chicken or turkey breast meat, the leanest cuts. And they call for removing the skin before cooking since this strips away even more of the fat.

Incidentally, while you'd get almost as much fat-reducing benefit from taking off the skin after cooking, there's a good reason to do this while the poultry is still raw. That way, the seasoning ingredients you add will flavor the meat—not the skin. and you'll have a much tastier dish.

Note that I've purposely not used ground turkey in any recipes. Often it includes dark meat and skin, which give it as much fat as ground beef.

CHICKEN CACCIATORE

*For a delicious company dinner, serve this traditional
Italian dish with a salad and crusty bread.*

4 Servings

Chicken and Vegetables

1 lb. skinless, boneless chicken breast meat, cut
    into 6 or 7 large pieces

¼ teaspoon salt (optional)

¼ teaspoon black pepper

1 tablespoon olive oil

1 large onion, chopped

8 ozs. fresh mushrooms, cleaned and sliced

2 garlic cloves, minced

½ cup defatted chicken broth, divided

1 tablespoon white flour

¼ cup dry sherry *or* white wine

1 cup canned tomatoes (preferably Italian-style),
    drained and chopped

1 large green bell pepper, seeded and cut into
    strips

½ teaspoon dried oregano leaves

½ teaspoon dried basil leaves

½ teaspoon dried thyme leaves
    Salt and pepper to taste (optional)

To Serve

1 8-oz. package thin spaghetti, cooked according
    to package directions

2 teaspoons grated Parmesan cheese per serving

Chicken and Vegetables:

Sprinkle chicken with salt, if desired, and pepper. In spray-coated Dutch oven or similar large, heavy pot, cook chicken pieces over medium heat, turning frequently, until they begin to brown. With slotted spoon, remove chicken to medium-sized bowl and set aside.

Add oil, onion, mushrooms, garlic, and 3 tablespoons broth to pot. Stir up any browned bits from pot bottom. Cook over medium heat, stirring frequently, 5 or 6 minutes or until onion is tender. If liquid begins to evaporate, add more broth.

Add flour and stir into a smooth paste. Stir in remaining chicken broth and sherry, and continue to stir until mixture thickens slightly. Add tomatoes, green pepper, oregano, basil, and thyme.

Return chicken to pot. Cover and simmer 30 minutes. Taste sauce and add additional salt and pepper if desired.

Serve individual portions of chicken and sauce over pasta. Top with Parmesan cheese.

Nutritional Data

PER SERVING		EXCHANGES	
Calories	463	Milk	0.0
Fat (gm)	8.3	Veg.	3.0
Sat. Fat (gm)	2.2	Fruit	0.0
Cholesterol (mg)	50	Bread	3.0
Sodium (mg)	302	Meat	3.0
Protein (gm)	29	Fat	0.0
Carbohydrate (gm)	60		
% Calories from fat	16		

POLENTA WITH CHICKEN, MUSHROOM, AND TOMATO SAUCE

◆

Polenta originated as Italian peasant fare, but it's easy to see why this cornmeal dish has become a staple of trendy restaurants— particularly when it's served with a flavorful sauce like this one, featuring chicken and mushrooms. The microwave makes quick and easy work of the cornmeal mixture. However, the recipe was designed using a high-powered microwave (900 w.). If yours has less power, you may need to lengthen the cooking time. For smooth-textured polenta, follow stirring directions carefully.

4-5 Servings

Sauce

- 3 tablespoons defatted chicken broth
- 2 teaspoons olive oil
- 1 medium-sized onion, chopped
- 2 garlic cloves, minced
- 8 ozs. fresh mushrooms, cleaned and sliced
- 1 large carrot, peeled and grated or shredded
- 2 14½-oz. cans Italian-style plum tomatoes, including juice, coarsely chopped
- 1 8-oz. can tomato sauce
- 2 tablespoons tomato paste
- 1 teaspoon granulated sugar
- 1 teaspoon dried basil leaves
- 1 teaspoon dried thyme leaves
- 1 teaspoon salt, or to taste (optional)
- ¼ teaspoon black pepper
- 3 large skinless chicken breast halves (about 2¼ lbs.), trimmed of all fat

Polenta

- 1⅓ cups yellow cornmeal
- 1 tablespoon granulated sugar
- ½ teaspoon salt, or to taste (optional)
- 3 cups water
- 1 cup 1% fat milk
- 1 medium onion, diced

Sauce: In Dutch oven or similar large, heavy pot, combine broth, oil, onion, garlic, and mushrooms. Cook over medium heat, stirring frequently, until onion is tender, 5 or 6 minutes. If liquid begins to evaporate, add a bit more broth. Add carrot, tomatoes, tomato sauce, tomato paste, sugar, basil, thyme, salt, if desired, and pepper; stir to mix well. Add chicken breasts.

Cover and bring to a boil. Reduce heat and simmer 35 to 40 minutes, stirring occasionally, until chicken is cooked through and flavors are well blended. Remove chicken. When cool enough to handle, cut into ½-inch strips and return to pot. Stir to mix well. Rewarm sauce when polenta is finished.

Polenta: After sauce has cooked 20 minutes, combine cornmeal, sugar, salt, if desired, water, milk, and onion in 2½-qt. microwave-safe casserole. Stir to mix well. Microwave, uncovered, on high power 8 to 9 minutes, stopping and stirring with wire whisk after 3 minutes and 6 minutes. After cooking, stir again with wire whisk until mixture is smooth. Cover with casserole lid and microwave an additional 6 to 7 minutes on high power. Remove from microwave and let stand an additional 3 to 4 minutes.

Serve individual portions of sauce over polenta.

Nutritional Data (based on 5 servings)

PER SERVING		EXCHANGES	
Calories	403	Milk	0.0
Fat (gm)	7.8	Veg.	3.0
Sat. Fat (gm)	1.9	Fruit	0.0
Cholesterol (mg)	85	Bread	1.5
Sodium (mg)	691	Meat	4.0
Protein (gm)	38	Fat	0.0
Carbohydrate (gm)	46		
% Calories from fat	17		

ARROZ CON POLLO

I first ordered this dish at the Spanish pavilion of the New York World's Fair in 1964 because it was one of the few items on the menu that I could translate—rice with chicken. I loved the combination of flavors, and the dish has been in my repertory ever since.

6-7 Servings

1 lb. boneless, skinless chicken breast meat, trimmed of all fat and cut into bite-sized pieces
2 teaspoons olive oil
1 large onion, chopped
2 garlic cloves, minced
2½ cups defatted chicken broth, divided
½ cup dry sherry
1 large green bell pepper, seeded and diced
1 large red bell pepper, seeded and diced (if unavailable, substitute yellow or green bell pepper)
¼ teaspoon saffron threads
¼ teaspoon black pepper
Dash cayenne pepper
1⅛ cups uncooked long-grain white rice
1½ cups green peas (fresh or frozen)

In spray-coated Dutch oven or similar large pot, cook chicken pieces over medium heat, turning frequently, 6 or 8 minutes, until they begin to brown and are cooked through. Remove and set aside in medium bowl.

In same pot, combine oil, onion, garlic, and 3 tablespoons broth. Stir up any brown bits from pan bottom. Cook over medium heat, stirring frequently, 6 or 7 minutes or until onion is tender. If liquid begins to evaporate, add a bit more broth.

Add remaining broth along with sherry, green and red peppers, and reserved chicken. Stir in saffron, black pepper, cayenne pepper, rice, and peas. Bring to a boil. Reduce heat and simmer 20 minutes or until rice is tender. Stir before serving.

Nutritional Data (based on 7 servings)

PER SERVING		EXCHANGES	
Calories	246	Milk	0.0
Fat (gm)	3.1	Veg.	1.0
Sat. Fat (gm)	1.0	Fruit	0.0
Cholesterol (mg)	30	Bread	2.0
Sodium (mg)	255	Meat	1.5
Protein (gm)	15	Fat	0.0
Carbohydrate (gm)	35		
% Calories from fat	12		

PAELLA

*A staple of Spanish cookery, paella was traditionally prepared
with whatever the cook had on hand, so it can be made with
a variety of ingredients. Often sausage was included, but
I've substituted Canadian bacon, which is far leaner but imparts
the flavor of smoked meat to the dish.*

4-5 Servings

½ lb. boneless, skinless chicken breast meat, trimmed of fat and cut into bite-sized pieces
2 teaspoons olive oil
1 large onion, chopped
2 garlic cloves, minced
2¾ cups reduced-sodium, defatted chicken broth *or* regular defatted chicken broth, divided
¼ teaspoon crushed saffron threads
1 14¼-oz. can Italian-style tomatoes, including juice
1 14¾-oz. jar water-packed artichoke hearts, drained
1 large red bell pepper, seeded and diced (if unavailable substitute green or yellow bell pepper)
1 large green bell pepper, seeded and diced
1 teaspoon dried thyme leaves
½ teaspoon dried basil leaves
⅛ teaspoon cayenne pepper
⅛ teaspoon black pepper
¼ lb. Canadian bacon, cut into thin strips
1¼ cups uncooked long-grain white rice
½ lb. medium shrimp, peeled and deveined
¼ teaspoon salt, or to taste (optional)

In spray-coated Dutch oven or similar large pot, cook chicken pieces over medium heat, turning frequently, 6 to 8 minutes or until they begin to brown. Remove and set aside in medium bowl.

In same pot, combine oil, onion, garlic, and 3 tablespoons broth. Stir up any brown bits from pan bottom. Cook over medium heat, stirring frequently, 6 to 7 minutes or until onion is tender. If liquid begins to evaporate, add a bit more broth.

Add saffron and remaining broth. Add tomatoes, breaking them up with large spoon, artichoke hearts, red pepper, green pepper, thyme, basil, cayenne pepper, black pepper, reserved chicken, and bacon.

Add rice. Bring to a boil. Cover, reduce heat, and simmer 15 minutes or until rice is almost tender. Add shrimp and cook an additional 5 to 6 minutes or until shrimp is curled and rice is tender. Add salt, if desired.

Stir before serving.

Nutritional Data (based on 5 servings)

PER SERVING		EXCHANGES	
Calories	371	Milk	0.0
Fat (gm)	4.6	Veg.	2.0
Sat. Fat (gm)	1.2	Fruit	0.0
Cholesterol (mg)	101	Bread	3.0
Sodium (mg)	678	Meat	2.0
Protein (gm)	28	Fat	0.0
Carbohydrate (gm)	56		
% Calories from fat	11		

CHICKEN RISOTTO

5 Servings

Chicken

¾ lb. boneless, skinless chicken breast meat, trimmed of all fat and cut into small bite-sized pieces

Risotto

¾ cup uncooked arborio rice

2 teaspoons olive oil

2⅔ cups defatted reduced-sodium chicken broth *or* defatted regular chicken broth

¼ teaspoon white pepper

Sauce and Garnish

1 medium onion, chopped

½ green bell pepper, seeded and diced

1 garlic clove, minced

2 teaspoons olive oil

3 tablespoons defatted reduced-sodium chicken broth *or* defatted regular chicken broth

¾ cup 1% fat milk

2 teaspoons Italian seasoning

2 tablespoons grated Parmesan cheese

Chicken: In large, non-stick, spray-coated skillet, cook chicken over medium heat until cooked through. Remove and set aside in medium bowl. Reserve skillet.

Risotto: In 2½-qt. microwave-safe casserole, combine rice and oil. Microwave, uncovered, 60 seconds on high power. Stir well. Add broth and pepper. Stir to mix well. Cover with casserole lid and microwave 6 to 7 minutes, turning casserole one-quarter turn during microwaving. Uncover, stir, and microwave an additional 11 to 12 minutes or until rice is tender and most of liquid is absorbed. Let stand 2 to 3 minutes.

Sauce and Garnish: Meanwhile, in skillet in which chicken was cooked, combine onion, green pepper, garlic, oil, and broth. Cook over medium heat, stirring frequently, until onion is tender, 5 to 6 minutes. Stir in milk, Italian seasoning, and reserved chicken. Cook, uncovered, over medium heat 3 or 4 minutes. Stir chicken mixture into risotto. Sprinkle with Parmesan cheese.

Nutritional Data

PER SERVING		EXCHANGES	
Calories	239	Milk	0.0
Fat (gm)	6.4	Veg.	0.5
Sat. Fat (gm)	1.6	Fruit	0.0
Cholesterol (mg)	31	Bread	2.0
Sodium (mg)	110	Meat	1.5
Protein (gm)	15	Fat	0.0
Carbohydrate (gm)	29		
% Calories from fat	25		

MIDDLE-EASTERN-STYLE CHICKEN

I love to serve dishes based on couscous. Not only does it cook quickly but it also lends a uniquely pleasing texture to one-pot meals. Like rice, this wheat product absorbs flavors readily—which makes it the perfect foil for the interesting blend of ingredients in this recipe.

5-6 Servings

1 lb. boneless, skinless chicken breast meat, trimmed of all fat and cut into 6 or 7 large pieces
1 large onion, chopped
2 garlic cloves, minced
2 teaspoons olive oil
1¾ cups defatted chicken broth
1 green bell pepper, seeded and diced
2 cups chopped fresh tomato
2 cups cooked garbanzo beans *or* 1 15-oz. can garbanzo beans, well drained
½ cup dark raisins
1 large bay leaf
1½ teaspoons dried thyme leaves
1 teaspoon ground cumin
¼ teaspoon ground allspice
⅛ teaspoon ground cloves
⅛ teaspoon black pepper
1 cup uncooked couscous
Salt to taste (optional)
Chopped parsley for garnish (optional)

In spray-coated Dutch oven or similar large, heavy pot, cook chicken pieces over medium heat, turning frequently, until they begin to brown. With slotted spoon, remove chicken to medium bowl and set aside.

To same pot, add onion, garlic, oil, and 2 tablespoons broth. Stir up any browned bits from bottom of pot. Cook over medium heat, stirring frequently, 5 or 6 minutes or until onion is tender. If liquid begins to evaporate, add more broth.

Return chicken to pot. Add remaining broth, green pepper, tomato, garbanzos, raisins, bay leaf, thyme, cumin, allspice, cloves, and black pepper. Bring to a boil, reduce heat, and simmer, covered, 20 to 25 minutes or until chicken is tender. Remove bay leaf and discard.

Add couscous and stir to mix well. Boil 2 minutes, covered. Remove pot from heat; stir up any couscous sticking to bottom. Allow mixture to stand 10 to 15 minutes, covered. Add salt to taste, if desired.

Arrange couscous on serving platter and top with chicken and sauce. Garnish with chopped parsley, if desired.

Nutritional Data (based on 6 servings)

PER SERVING		EXCHANGES	
Calories	389	Milk	0.0
Fat (gm)	5.4	Veg.	1.0
Sat. Fat (gm)	1	Fruit	1.0
Cholesterol (mg)	34	Bread	3.0
Sodium (mg)	235	Meat	1.5
Protein (gm)	24	Fat	0.0
Carbohydrate (gm)	63		
% Calories from fat	12		

TARRAGON-MUSTARD CHICKEN

Tarragon and mustard team up to give this chicken its tangy flavor.

5-6 Servings

- 1 lb. boneless, skinless chicken breast meat, trimmed of all fat
- 2½ teaspoons dried tarragon leaves, divided
- ½ teaspoon salt (optional)
- 2 teaspoons olive oil
- 1 cup chopped onion
- 2 large celery stalks, chopped
- 1½ cups defatted chicken broth, divided
- 2 tablespoons Dijon-style mustard
- 2 teaspoons, packed, light brown sugar
- 1 teaspoon lemon juice
- ⅛ teaspoon white pepper
- ⅛ teaspoon salt, or to taste (optional)
- ¼ cup water
- 2 teaspoons cornstarch
- 1¼ cups uncooked long-grain white rice, cooked according to package directions

Cut chicken into small bite-sized pieces. Sprinkle with ½ teaspoon tarragon and salt, if desired. In large, non-stick, spray-coated skillet, cook chicken pieces over medium heat, turning frequently with large wooden or plastic spoon, 7 to 10 minutes or until they begin to brown and are cooked through. Remove and set aside in medium bowl.

In skillet in which chicken was cooked, combine oil, onion, celery, and 3 tablespoons broth. Cook over medium heat, stirring frequently, 6 or 7 minutes or until onion is tender. If liquid begins to evaporate, add a bit more broth.

Add mustard to pan and stir to combine well. Stir in remaining chicken broth, brown sugar, remaining tarragon, lemon juice, white pepper, and salt, if desired. Stir in reserved chicken. Cover and simmer 20 minutes or until flavors are blended. Bring to a boil.

Combine water and cornstarch in a cup. Stir into sauce and cook, stirring, until thickened. Simmer an additional 2 or 3 minutes.

Arrange rice on large serving platter. Top with chicken and sauce. Or serve individual portions of chicken and sauce over rice.

Nutritional Data (based on 6 servings)

PER SERVING		EXCHANGES	
Calories	247	Milk	0.0
Fat (gm)	3.8	Veg.	0.5
Sat. Fat (gm)	0.8	Fruit	0.0
Cholesterol (mg)	30	Bread	2.0
Sodium (mg)	193	Meat	1.5
Protein (gm)	16	Fat	0.0
Carbohydrate (gm)	37		
% Calories from fat	14		

CARIBBEAN-STYLE CHICKEN WITH BLACK BEANS

◆

The flavors of the islands come alive in this chicken and black bean skillet dinner.

4-6 Servings

- 1 lb. boneless, skinless chicken breast halves, trimmed of all fat
- ¼ teaspoon salt (optional)
- ¼ teaspoon black pepper
- 2 teaspoons non-diet, tub-style margarine *or* butter
- 1 medium-sized onion, chopped
- 2 garlic cloves, minced
- 1 cup defatted chicken broth, divided
- 1¼ cups uncooked long-grain white rice
- 1 8-oz. can tomato sauce
- ¼ cup light rum
- 1 green bell pepper, seeded and diced
- ½ teaspoon ground cinnamon
- ¼ teaspoon ground cloves
- ¼ teaspoon salt, or to taste (optional)
    Dash cayenne pepper (optional)
- 2 cups cooked black beans *or* 1 16-oz. can black beans, well drained

Sprinkle chicken with salt, if using, and pepper. In large non-stick, spray-coated skillet, cook chicken over medium heat 8 to 10 minutes or until pieces have begun to brown. Remove to medium bowl and reserve. When chicken is cool enough to handle, cut into small strips.

In same skillet, melt margarine. Add onion, garlic, and 2 tablespoons broth and cook 5 or 6 minutes or until onion is soft, stirring frequently.

Meanwhile, cook rice according to package directions.

To skillet, add tomato sauce, remaining chicken broth, and rum. Stir to mix well. Add green pepper, reserved chicken, cinnamon, cloves, salt, if desired, and cayenne pepper, if desired. Bring to a boil. Reduce heat and simmer, uncovered, 15 minutes or until chicken is tender and liquid has thickened.

Stir in beans, and heat 2 or 3 minutes longer.

To serve, place rice on large platter and top with chicken and bean mixture. Or serve individual portions over rice.

Nutritional Data (based on 6 servings)

PER SERVING		EXCHANGES	
Calories	336	Milk	0.0
Fat (gm)	3.4	Veg.	0.5
Sat. Fat (gm)	1.0	Fruit	0.0
Cholesterol (mg)	32	Bread	3.0
Sodium (mg)	390	Meat	2.0
Protein (gm)	20	Fat	0.0
Carbohydrate (gm)	50		
% Calories from fat	9		

CHICKEN AND BULGUR STIR-FRY

Bulgur wheat, a Middle-Eastern grain product, adds a nutty flavor and chewy texture to this chicken skillet dish. Soaking the grain in hot water first speeds its cooking.

4-5 Servings

¾ cup uncooked bulgur wheat

1 lb. boneless, skinless chicken breast meat, trimmed of all fat and cut into bite-sized pieces

¼ teaspoon salt (optional)

⅛ teaspoon black pepper

2 teaspoons olive oil

3 cups mixed frozen red, green, and yellow bell peppers

2 garlic cloves, minced

1⅓ cups fat-free, reduced-sodium chicken broth *or* regular defatted chicken broth, divided

2 teaspoons chili powder

2 teaspoons paprika

1 teaspoon dried thyme leaves

¼ cup finely chopped fresh parsley leaves

¼ cup finely chopped fresh chives *or* sliced green onion tops

In a 4-cup measure or similar medium bowl, combine bulgur and 1½ cups hot water and set aside.

Sprinkle chicken with salt, if desired, and pepper. In a large non-stick skillet coated with non-stick spray, cook chicken pieces over medium heat, stirring frequently, 7 to 10 minutes or until chicken begins to brown and is cooked through. Remove and set aside in a medium bowl.

In skillet in which chicken was cooked, combine oil, peppers, garlic, and 3 tablespoons of broth. Cook over medium heat, stirring frequently, 4 to 5 minutes or until peppers are tender. If liquid begins to evaporate, add a bit more broth.

Add remaining broth along with chili powder, paprika, and thyme. Return reserved chicken to skillet. Bring to a boil. Cover, lower heat, and simmer 10 minutes.

Drain bulgur in a large sieve. Add bulgur, parsley, and chives to chicken mixture. Stir to mix well. Bring to a boil. Lower heat and simmer, uncovered, an additional 10 minutes, stirring frequently, until bulgur is tender and most of liquid is absorbed.

Nutritional Data (based on 5 servings)

PER SERVING		EXCHANGES	
Calories	257	Milk	0.0
Fat (gm)	5.2	Veg.	2.0
Sat. Fat (gm)	1	Fruit	0.0
Cholesterol (mg)	55.2	Bread	1.0
Sodium (mg)	153	Meat	2.5
Protein (gm)	26.6	Fat	0.0
Carbohydrate (gm)	28.6		
% Calories from fat	17		

BARBECUED CHICKEN AND VEGETABLES OVER POTATOES

————————◆————————

Shredded cabbage adds texture to this tangy, no-fuss, microwave potato topper. The chicken and sauce also make a great open-faced sandwich on English muffins or rolls.

4-5 Servings

1½ cups finely shredded cabbage
2 cups chopped onion
1 garlic clove, minced
1 lb. boneless, skinless chicken breast meat, trimmed of all fat and cut into thin strips
1 8-oz. can reduced-sodium tomato sauce *or* regular tomato sauce
½ cup ketchup
1 sweet red, *or* green, bell pepper, seeded and diced
1 tablespoon granulated sugar
2 teaspoons balsamic vinegar
1 teaspoon dried thyme leaves
¼ teaspoon powdered mustard
⅛ teaspoon ground cloves

3-4 drops hot pepper sauce

4-5 large baking potatoes, oven or microwave-
baked

Combine cabbage, onion, and garlic in 2½-qt. microwave-safe casserole.
Cover with casserole lid and microwave on high power 4 to 5 minutes, or
until onions and cabbage are partially cooked, turning casserole and stirring mixture once during microwaving.

Add chicken, tomato sauce, ketchup, bell pepper, sugar, vinegar, thyme,
mustard, cloves, and hot pepper sauce. Stir to mix well. Cover and
microwave 5 to 7 minutes on high power, turning casserole one-quarter
turn and stirring contents once during microwaving.

Serve chicken and sauce over baked potatoes.

Nutritional Data (based on 5 servings)

PER SERVING		EXCHANGES	
Calories	282	Milk	0.0
Fat (gm)	2.0	Veg.	2.0
Sat. Fat (gm)	0.5	Fruit	0.0
Cholesterol (mg)	37	Bread	2.0
Sodium (mg)	383	Meat	1.5
Protein (gm)	18	Fat	0.0
Carbohydrate (gm)	49		
% Calories from fat	6		

CHICKEN WITH DRIED FRUIT

Dried prunes and apricots make a wonderfully sweet sauce for chicken.

4-5 Servings

1 lb. boneless, skinless chicken breast meat, trimmed of all fat and cut into bite-sized pieces
¼ teaspoon salt (optional)
⅛ teaspoon black pepper
1 large onion, chopped
1 garlic clove, minced
2 teaspoons olive oil
1 cup defatted chicken broth, divided
¼ cup light rum
1½ cups mixed dried pitted prunes and apricots (about 9 ozs. fruit)
½ red bell pepper, seeded and diced
½ teaspoon ground ginger
1 large bay leaf
1¼ cups uncooked long-grain white rice
Additional apricots for garnish (optional)

Sprinkle chicken with salt, if desired, and pepper. In large, non-stick, spray-coated skillet, cook chicken over medium heat until meat turns white, 6 to 7 minutes. Remove to medium bowl and reserve.

In same skillet, cook onion and garlic in oil and 3 tablespoons broth until onion is tender, about 5 or 6 minutes. If liquid begins to evaporate, add more broth. Add remaining broth, rum, fruit, red pepper, ginger, and bay leaf. Stir to mix well.

Stir in reserved chicken. Bring to a boil. Cover, reduce heat, and cook 20 minutes or until flavors are well blended. Remove bay leaf. Uncover skillet, raise heat, and cook, stirring frequently, until sauce has thickened slightly.

Meanwhile, cook rice according to package directions.

Arrange rice on serving platter, and top with fruit and chicken mixture. Garnish with additional apricots, if desired.

Nutritional Data (based on 5 servings)

PER SERVING		EXCHANGES	
Calories	406	Milk	0.0
Fat (gm)	4.2	Veg.	1.0
Sat. Fat (gm)	0.8	Fruit	2.0
Cholesterol (mg)	36	Bread	2.5
Sodium (mg)	105	Meat	1.5
Protein (gm)	19	Fat	0.0
Carbohydrate (gm)	68		
% Calories from fat	9		

CHICKEN-FRIED RICE

This is a great way to use leftover cooked chicken, with a bonus: the flavorful "fried rice" has very little fat. The brown sauce, five-spice powder, and rice vinegar are common oriental seasonings available at larger grocery stores and specialty markets.

5-6 Servings

- 3 cups water
- 3 tablespoons reduced-sodium soy sauce
- 1 teaspoon five-spice powder
- ¼ teaspoon salt (optional)
- ⅛ teaspoon red pepper flakes
- 1½ cups uncooked long-grain white rice
- 3 tablespoons defatted chicken broth
- 2 teaspoons sesame oil
- 4 cups thinly sliced bok choy leaves and stems
- 1 red bell pepper, seeded and diced
- ¼ cup thinly sliced green onion
- 1 *cooked* skinless, boneless chicken breast (8 to 9 ozs.), cut into small cubes
- 1 8-oz. can sliced water chestnuts, well drained
- 2 teaspoons brown sauce
- 2 teaspoons rice vinegar

In medium saucepan, stir together water, soy sauce, five-spice powder, salt, if desired, and red pepper flakes. Add rice. Cover and bring to a boil. Reduce heat and cook 20 minutes or until water is absorbed and rice is tender.

When rice is done, combine broth and oil in large, non-stick skillet. Add bok choy, red pepper, and green onion and cook over medium-high heat, stirring, 2 to 3 minutes. Add cooked rice, cooked chicken, water chestnuts, brown sauce, and vinegar and cook an additional 3 to 4 minutes or until flavors are well blended.

Nutritional Data (based on 6 servings)

PER SERVING		EXCHANGES	
Calories	252	Milk	0.0
Fat (gm)	2.7	Veg.	1.0
Sat. Fat (gm)	0.5	Fruit	0.0
Cholesterol (mg)	15	Bread	2.5
Sodium (mg)	393	Meat	1.0
Protein (gm)	11	Fat	0.0
Carbohydrate (gm)	45		
% Calories from fat	10		

HONEY-MUSTARD CHICKEN

The honey-mustard flavor of this delicious chicken recipe is sparked by the addition of a little curry powder.

5-6 Servings

    1 lb. boneless, skinless chicken breast meat, trimmed of all fat
    ½ teaspoon salt (optional)
    ⅛ teaspoon black pepper
    2 teaspoons olive oil
    1 cup chopped onion
    1¾ cups fat-free, reduced-sodium chicken broth *or* regular chicken broth, divided
    2 tablespoons mild honey, such as clover
    1 tablespoon Dijon-style mustard
    1 teaspoon mild curry powder
    2 cups small cauliflower florets
    1 large carrot, peeled and thinly sliced
    1¼ cups uncooked long-grain white rice, cooked according to package directions

Cut chicken into small bite-sized pieces. Sprinkle with ½ teaspoon salt, if desired, and pepper. In a large non-stick skillet coated with non-stick spray, cook chicken pieces over medium heat, turning frequently with a large wooden or plastic spoon, 7 to 10 minutes or until they begin to brown and are cooked through. Remove and set aside in a medium bowl.

In skillet in which chicken was cooked, combine oil, onion, and 3 table-spoons of broth. Cook over medium heat, stirring frequently, 6 to 7 min-utes or until onion is tender. If liquid begins to evaporate, add a bit more broth.

Add honey, mustard, and curry powder to pan with onion, and stir to mix well. Stir in remaining broth. Stir in reserved chicken, cauliflower, and car-rot. Bring to a boil. Cover, reduce heat, and simmer 10 minutes. Remove cover and simmer an additional 5 to 7 minutes or until sauce has reduced by half.

Arrange rice on a large serving platter. Top with chicken and sauce. Or serve individual portions over rice.

Nutritional Data (based on 6 servings)

PER SERVING		EXCHANGES	
Calories	299	Milk	0.0
Fat (gm)	4	Veg.	1.0
Sat. Fat (gm)	0.9	Fruit	0.0
Cholesterol (mg)	46	Bread	2.5
Sodium (mg)	188	Meat	2.0
Protein (gm)	22.2	Fat	0.0
Carbohydrate (gm)	42.5		
% Calories from fat	12		

"STUFFED" CHICKEN BREASTS

Here's baked chicken and stuffing—with only a fraction of the fat and all the flavor.

4-6 Servings

Stuffing

- 1 tablespoon non-diet, tub-style margarine *or* butter
- 2 cups chopped onion
- 2 large celery stalks, diced
- 2 small carrots, diced
- 2 tablespoons chopped fresh parsley leaves
- 1 cup defatted chicken broth, divided
- ½ teaspoon poultry seasoning
- ⅛ teaspoon black pepper
- 3½ cups *seasoned* commercial cube-style stuffing

Chicken

- 4-6 large bone-in chicken breast halves (2½-3 lbs.), skin removed and trimmed of all fat
- 1 teaspoon non-diet, tub-style margarine *or* butter
- 1½ teaspoons poultry seasoning
- ¼ teaspoon salt (optional)
- ⅛ teaspoon black pepper

Garnish

Parsley sprigs (optional)

Preheat oven to 350° F.

Stuffing: In large, non-stick skillet, combine margarine, onion, celery, carrot, parsley, and 3 tablespoons broth. Cook over medium heat, stirring frequently, until onion is tender, about 6 or 7 minutes. If liquid begins to evaporate, add a bit more broth. Stir in poultry seasoning and black pepper. Add stuffing and remaining broth. Stir to mix well. Transfer to 9½x13-inch baking pan coated with non-stick spray.

Chicken: Place breasts over stuffing, bone side down. Spread margarine over chicken. Sprinkle evenly with poultry seasoning, salt, if desired, and black pepper. Bake 20 minutes. Move chicken to side of pan, and stir stuffing. Rearrange chicken over stuffing, and bake an additional 30 to 35 minutes or until chicken is cooked through.

Transfer stuffing to serving platter, and arrange chicken on top. Or serve individual portions of chicken over stuffing.

Garnish: Sprinkle with parsley sprigs, if desired.

Nutritional Data (based on 6 servings)

PER SERVING		EXCHANGES	
Calories	274	Milk	0.0
Fat (gm)	6.5	Veg.	1.0
Sat. Fat (gm)	1.4	Fruit	0.0
Cholesterol (mg)	76.2	Bread	1.0
Sodium (mg)	406	Meat	3.0
Protein (gm)	32	Fat	0.0
Carbohydrate (gm)	20.7		
% Calories from fat	22		

CHICKEN AND ESCAROLE SOUP WITH ORZO

In salads, escarole can be bitter. Cooked, it takes on a completely different character. So give this unusual soup a try. It's delicious. For texture and body, I've added a rice-shaped pasta called orzo.

5-6 Servings

1 lb. boneless, skinless chicken breast meat, trimmed of all fat and cut into bite-sized pieces
2 teaspoons olive oil
1 large onion, chopped
1 garlic clove, minced
6 cups defatted chicken broth, divided
1 14½-oz. can tomatoes (preferably Italian-style), including juice, chopped
3 cups trimmed, washed, and thinly sliced escarole
1 medium-sized rutabaga, peeled and finely diced
1 large carrot, peeled and chopped
½ cup uncooked orzo
¼ teaspoon black pepper
   Salt to taste (optional)

In non-stick, spray-coated Dutch oven or similar large heavy pot, cook chicken over medium heat, stirring frequently, until pieces begin to brown. Remove and reserve.

In same pot, combine oil, onion, garlic, and 3 tablespoons broth. Scrape up any brown bits of chicken from pot bottom. Cook onion and garlic over medium heat, stirring frequently, until onion is tender, about 5 to 6 minutes. If liquid begins to evaporate, add more broth.

Add remaining broth, along with tomatoes, reserved chicken, escarole, rutabaga, carrot, orzo, and pepper. Bring to a boil. Cover, reduce heat, and simmer 15 to 18 minutes or until orzo is cooked and rutabaga is tender. Add salt to taste, if desired.

Nutritional Data (based on 6 servings)

PER SERVING		EXCHANGES	
Calories	171	Milk	0.0
Fat (gm)	4.4	Veg.	1.0
Sat. Fat (gm)	1.8	Fruit	0.0
Cholesterol (mg)	42	Bread	1.0
Sodium (mg)	793	Meat	1.5
Protein (gm)	16	Fat	0.0
Carbohydrate (gm)	17		
% Calories from fat	23		

ARTICHOKE "STUFFED" TURKEY

---◆---

Skinless turkey cutlets are so low in fat that you'll want to use them often. Here's a tasty variation of "stuffed" turkey that you can make in a jiffy in a skillet. To save time, the stuffing is made with purchased, seasoned crumb-style stuffing mix, which absorbs liquid more evenly than cube-style. After the stuffing is prepared, it's removed to a serving platter and kept warm while the turkey is quickly cooked.

4-5 Servings

Stuffing

- 2 teaspoons non-diet, tub-style margarine *or* butter
- ½ cup defatted chicken broth, divided
- 1 cup chopped onion
- 1 large celery stalk, diced
- 1 garlic clove, minced
- 1 14½-oz. can reduced-sodium tomatoes *or* regular tomatoes, drained and coarsely chopped
- 1 14¾-oz. jar water-packed artichoke hearts, drained and coarsely chopped
- ¼ cup finely chopped parsley leaves
- ½ teaspoon dried basil leaves
- ½ teaspoon dried thyme leaves
- ¼ teaspoon salt, or to taste (optional)
- ⅛ teaspoon black pepper
- 1½ cups *seasoned* commercial crumb-style stuffing

Turkey

- 2 teaspoons non-diet, tub-style margarine *or* butter
- ½ teaspoon salt (optional)
- ¼ teaspoon black pepper
- 1 lb. uncooked turkey breast cutlets

To Serve

- Parsley sprigs for garnish (optional)

Stuffing: Preheat oven to 200° F. In large, non-stick skillet, combine margarine, 3 tablespoons broth, onion, celery, and garlic. Cook over medium heat 5 or 6 minutes, stirring frequently, until onion is tender. If liquid begins to evaporate, add a bit more broth.

Add remaining broth, along with tomatoes, artichoke hearts, parsley, basil, thyme, salt, if desired, and black pepper. Stir to combine well. Bring to a boil. Cook, uncovered, 3 to 4 minutes or until liquid has thickened and only about ¼ cup remains.

Stir in stuffing mix. Reduce heat and cook an additional 2 minutes, stirring frequently. Remove stuffing to serving platter, and keep warm in oven while turkey cooks.

Turkey: Rinse out and dry pan in which stuffing was cooked. Melt margarine in pan over medium heat. Sprinkle salt, if desired, and pepper evenly over turkey.

In batches, add turkey to pan and cook over medium heat until cooked through, about 2 minutes per side. Do not overcook.

To Serve: Arrange turkey cutlets on serving platter over stuffing. Garnish with parsley, if desired.

Nutritional Data (based on 5 servings)

PER SERVING		EXCHANGES	
Calories	228	Milk	0.0
Fat (gm)	5.9	Veg.	3.0
Sat. Fat (gm)	1.3	Fruit	0.0
Cholesterol (mg)	41	Bread	0.5
Sodium (mg)	360	Meat	2.0
Protein (gm)	23	Fat	0.0
Carbohydrate (gm)	23		
% Calories from fat	22		

CRANBERRY AND APPLE "STUFFED" TURKEY

You don't have to wait until Thanksgiving to enjoy a platter of sliced turkey with stuffing. This tasty version is both quick and easy and includes cranberries and apples along with the onions and celery. The recipe uses seasoned commercial crumb-style stuffing, as it absorbs liquid more easily than cube-type stuffing.

5-6 Servings

Stuffing

- 2 teaspoons non-diet, tub-style margarine *or* butter
- ½ cup defatted chicken broth, divided
- 1 large, tart apple, cored and cubed
- 1 cup chopped onion
- 1 large celery stalk, diced
- 1 cup whole berry cranberry sauce
- ¾ teaspoon poultry seasoning
- ¼ teaspoon salt, or to taste (optional)
- 2 cups *seasoned* commercial crumb-style stuffing

Turkey

- 2 teaspoons non-diet, tub-style margarine *or* butter
- ½ teaspoon poultry seasoning
- 1½ lbs. uncooked turkey breast cutlets

To Serve

Parsley sprigs and additional cranberry sauce for garnish (optional)

Stuffing: Preheat oven to 200° F. In large, non-stick skillet, combine margarine, 3 tablespoons broth, apple, onion, and celery. Cook over medium heat 6 or 7 minutes, stirring frequently, until onion is tender. If liquid begins to evaporate, add a bit more broth.

Add remaining broth, along with cranberry sauce, poultry seasoning, and salt, if desired. Stir to mix well. Bring to a boil. Cook, uncovered, 2 or 3 minutes or until liquid has thickened slightly.

Stir in stuffing mix. Reduce heat and cook an additional 2 minutes, stirring frequently. Remove stuffing to serving platter, and keep warm in oven while turkey cooks.

Turkey: Rinse out and dry pan in which stuffing was cooked. Melt margarine in pan over medium heat. Sprinkle poultry seasoning evenly over turkey.

In batches, add turkey to pan and cook over medium heat until cooked through, about 2 minutes per side. Do not overcook.

To Serve: Arrange stuffing on large serving platter or on individual plates. Top with turkey. Garnish with parsley and/or additional cranberry sauce, if desired.

Nutritional Data (based on 6 servings)

PER SERVING		EXCHANGES	
Calories	261	Milk	0.0
Fat (gm)	5.5	Veg.	1.0
Sat. Fat (gm)	1.3	Fruit	1.0
Cholesterol (mg)	44	Bread	1.0
Sodium (mg)	249	Meat	2.0
Protein (gm)	21.6	Fat	0.0
Carbohydrate (gm)	31.6		
% Calories from fat	19		

GINGER TURKEY STIR-FRY

Here's a colorful oriental stir-fry in which I've substituted turkey breast for the more traditional chicken. The switch works well because the marinade gives the turkey a surprising amount of flavor. However, the recipe could also be made with bite-sized chicken breast pieces if you prefer. The "hot oil" is a common spicy oriental seasoning.

4-5 Servings

½ cup defatted chicken broth, divided
¼ cup dry sherry
2 tablespoons reduced-sodium soy sauce
1 tablespoon brown sugar
2 teaspoons rice vinegar
1 teaspoon chopped fresh ginger *or* ½ teaspoon ground ginger
2-3 drops "hot oil"
1 lb. turkey breast cutlets, cut into thin strips
1⅓ cups uncooked long-grain white rice
2 teaspoons sesame oil
1 large onion, chopped
1 clove garlic, minced
1 large carrot, peeled and grated or shredded
1 large celery stalk, sliced diagonally
½ large red bell pepper, seeded and cut into ¾-in. squares
2 cups small broccoli *or* cauliflower florets
2 cups sliced bok choy leaves and stems

In medium bowl, combine 2 tablespoons chicken broth, sherry, soy sauce, brown sugar, vinegar, ginger, and hot oil. Stir to mix well. Add turkey. Stir to coat. Refrigerate and marinate 20 to 30 minutes, stirring occasionally.

Cook rice according to package directions.

Remove turkey from marinade with slotted spoon. Reserve marinade in refrigerator. In large, non-stick, spray-coated skillet, quickly cook turkey pieces over medium heat, stirring frequently, until turkey changes color. Remove to medium bowl and reserve.

Add sesame oil to skillet, along with 2 tablespoons of reserved marinade from turkey. Add onion and garlic and cook over medium heat 4 or 5 minutes, stirring frequently. Add carrot, celery, red pepper, remaining marinade, and remaining broth. Cook an additional 2 to 3 minutes, stirring frequently.

Add broccoli and bok choy. Cook an additional 5 minutes or until broccoli is almost tender. Return turkey to pan and cook an additional 1 to 2 minutes per side or until turkey changes color.

Serve turkey and vegetables over rice on serving platter.

Nutritional Data (based on 5 servings)

PER SERVING		EXCHANGES	
Calories	271	Milk	0.0
Fat (gm)	4.1	Veg.	2.0
Sat. Fat (gm)	0.9	Fruit	0.0
Cholesterol (mg)	40	Bread	1.5
Sodium (mg)	340	Meat	2.0
Protein (gm)	22	Fat	0.0
Carbohydrate (gm)	33		
% Calories from fat	14		

4
FISH AND SEAFOOD

O ne good way to slash the fat in your diet is to eat fish several times
a week. Try some of the appealing recipes in this chapter such as
Spicy Shrimp and Rice, Manhattan-Style Clam Chowder, and Cajun
Fish. Most feature shellfish, which are very lean (clams have only 1 gram of
fat in a 3-ounce serving; shrimp 2 grams), or low-fat but tasty fish such as
flounder, haddock, sole, hake, and yellowfin tuna (which have 1 to 3 grams
of fat in a 3-ounce serving). But I've also included salmon, which is a high-
er-fat selection, because it's such a popular and flavorful choice. Salmon is
also a good source of omega 3 acids, which have been shown to lower
blood cholesterol.

SEAFOOD RISOTTO, MILANESE STYLE

In my tireless search for great risotto recipes for this book, I tasted examples in world-class Italian restaurants from California to Maryland. This one's freely adapted from a dish I had in St.Louis. Although I've cut the fat considerably, the results are rich and delicious. Risotto is made with arborio rice (available at specialty markets and many grocery stores), which gives the dish its characteristic creamy texture. Made on top of the stove, it needs almost constant stirring—but not with the microwave. The recipe was tested in a high-powered microwave (900 w.). If yours has less power, you may need to lengthen the cooking time.

4-6 Servings

Risotto

- ¾ cup uncooked arborio rice
- 2 teaspoons non-diet, tub-style margarine *or* butter
- 2⅔ cups defatted reduced-sodium chicken broth *or* defatted regular chicken broth
- ½ teaspoon dried thyme leaves
- ¼ teaspoon white pepper

Seafood and Sauce

- 1 medium onion, chopped
- 1 garlic clove, minced
- 2 teaspoons non-diet, tub-style margarine *or* butter
- ⅓ cup defatted reduced-sodium chicken broth *or* defatted regular chicken broth
- ¼ teaspoon crushed saffron threads
- ½ lb. bay scallops
- ½ lb. medium shrimp, uncooked, peeled, and deveined
- 1 cup diced zucchini
- 3 tablespoons grated Parmesan cheese

Risotto: In 2½-quart microwave-safe casserole, combine rice and margarine. Microwave, uncovered, 60 seconds on high power. Stir well. Add broth, thyme, and pepper. Stir to mix well. Cover with casserole lid and microwave 7 to 8 minutes, turning casserole one-quarter turn during microwaving. Uncover, stir well, and microwave an additional 11 to 13 minutes or until most of liquid is absorbed and rice is tender. Allow to stand 2 to 3 minutes.

Seafood and Sauce: Meanwhile, in large, non-stick skillet, combine onion, garlic, margarine, broth, and saffron. Cook over medium heat, stirring frequently, until onion is tender, about 5 to 6 minutes. Stir in scallops, shrimp, and zucchini. Cook, uncovered, over medium heat 3 or 4 minutes, stirring frequently. Stir mixture into cooked risotto. Stir in Parmesan cheese.

Nutritional Data (based on 6 servings)

PER SERVING		EXCHANGES	
Calories	214	Milk	0.0
Fat (gm)	4.7	Veg.	0.0
Sat. Fat (gm)	1.2	Fruit	0.0
Cholesterol (mg)	81	Bread	1.5
Sodium (mg)	277	Meat	2.0
Protein (gm)	19	Fat	0.0
Carbohydrate (gm)	23		
% Calories from fat	20		

"CREAMY" SALMON OVER PASTA

I fell in love with this opulent pasta dish on my first trip to Italy. Here's my slimmed down but rich-tasting interpretation, which makes a wonderful company meal. The recipe includes non-fat sour cream, lending creaminess without adding fat.

5-6 Servings

- ¾ lb. Atlantic salmon fillet or steaks, cut into 2-in. pieces
- 1 large onion, finely chopped
- 1 large carrot, peeled and grated or shredded
- 1 small garlic clove, minced
- 3 tablespoons defatted chicken broth
- 1 tablespoon non-diet, tub-style margarine *or* butter
- 2 tablespoons white flour
- 1¾ cups 1% fat milk
- 2 tablespoons dry sherry
- 1 teaspoon lemon juice
- ½ teaspoon dried dill weed
- ½ teaspoon dry mustard
- ⅛ teaspoon white pepper
- ⅓ cup non-fat sour cream
  Salt to taste (optional)
- 8-10 ozs. thin spaghetti, cooked according to package directions
  Chopped parsley for garnish (optional)

Remove skin from salmon. In large, non-stick, spray-coated skillet, cook salmon, breaking up large pieces, until cooked through, about 11 to 12 minutes. Remove from pan and set aside.

In same pan, combine onion, carrot, garlic, broth, and margarine. Cook over medium heat, stirring frequently, 6 to 7 minutes or until onion is tender.

Mix in flour and stir to make a smooth paste. Gradually add milk, stirring constantly to make sure mixture remains smooth. Add sherry, lemon juice, dill, mustard, and pepper. Simmer 3 or 4 minutes longer, stirring frequently, until sauce thickens.

Meanwhile, flake salmon and fold into sauce. Stir in sour cream. Cook over very low heat an additional 3 or 4 minutes.

Arrange pasta on serving platter. Top with salmon and sauce. Or serve individual portions over pasta. Garnish with chopped parsley, if desired.

Nutritional Data (based on 6 servings)

PER SERVING		EXCHANGES	
Calories	325	Milk	0.5
Fat (gm)	7.2	Veg.	0.5
Sat. Fat (gm)	1.5	Fruit	0.0
Cholesterol (mg)	35	Bread	2.0
Sodium (mg)	112	Meat	2.0
Protein (gm)	20	Fat	0.5
Carbohydrate (gm)	42		
% Calories from fat	20		

LAYERED SALMON AND VEGETABLES

Here's an interesting variation on the one-pot concept—a layered fish stew. The vegetables go in first, and the fish steams on top. Thick fillets will take a bit longer to cook than thinner ones. The cubanel pepper called for is an elongated yellow-green pepper that looks as if it should be hot. However, its distinctive flavor does not rely on "heat."

4-5 Servings

1 lb. small boiling potatoes, peeled or unpeeled, cut into ½-in. cubes (about 3 generous cups)
3 carrots, peeled and sliced
1 medium onion, finely chopped
3 plum tomatoes, chopped
1 cubanel pepper, seeded and chopped, *or* green bell pepper
¼ cup chopped parsley leaves
2 teaspoons chopped fresh dill weed *or* 1 teaspoon dried dill weed, divided
2 garlic cloves, minced
¾ teaspoon salt (optional)
¼ teaspoon black pepper
¾ cup defatted chicken broth
2 teaspoons lemon juice
2 teaspoons olive oil

1 lb. salmon fillets
Additional chopped dill weed for garnish
Additional salt and pepper (optional)

Arrange potato cubes evenly on bottom of spray-coated Dutch oven or similar large, heavy pot. Add carrot slices in even layer, followed by onion, chopped tomatoes, and cubanel pepper. Sprinkle with parsley, 1 teaspoon fresh dill weed (or ½ teaspoon dried), garlic, salt, if using, and pepper.

In small bowl, combine broth, lemon juice, and oil. Pour over vegetables. Lay salmon over vegetables, skin side down. Sprinkle with 1 teaspoon fresh dill weed (or ½ teaspoon dried).

Bring to a boil. Cover, lower heat, and simmer 18 to 25 minutes or until fish is almost cooked through. Remove lid and continue to cook until liquid is somewhat reduced and concentrated in flavor and potatoes are tender, about 10 to 15 minutes longer.

Remove salmon to serving platter. Remove salmon skin. Sprinkle with additional dill, salt, and pepper, if desired. Surround fish with vegetables and liquid.

Nutritional Data (based on 5 servings)

PER SERVING		EXCHANGES	
Calories	264	Milk	0.0
Fat (gm)	8.2	Veg.	1.0
Sat. Fat (gm)	1.4	Fruit	0.0
Cholesterol (mg)	52	Bread	1.5
Sodium (mg)	153	Meat	2.5
Protein (gm)	21	Fat	0.0
Carbohydrate (gm)	27		
% Calories from fat	28		

SPICY SHRIMP AND RICE

After enjoying some wonderful seafood combinations down in the bayou country of Louisiana, I came home anxious to experiment with reduced-fat dishes that would capture the flavor of that region. Here's a full-bodied shrimp and rice hot pot that's seasoned with a creative combination of spices.

7-8 Servings

2 teaspoons olive oil
1 large onion, chopped
2 large garlic cloves, minced
2¼ cups defatted chicken broth *or* bouillon, divided
2 large celery stalks, diced
1 large carrot, peeled and diced
1 large green bell pepper, seeded and chopped
1 14½-oz. can reduced-sodium diced tomatoes, including juice, *or* regular canned diced tomatoes
1 large bay leaf
1½ teaspoons dried thyme leaves
¾ teaspoon chili powder
½ teaspoon paprika
⅛ teaspoon salt, or to taste (optional)
¼ teaspoon black pepper
Dash cayenne pepper (optional)
1½ cups uncooked long-grain white rice
1 lb. medium shrimp, uncooked, peeled, and deveined

In large, heavy pot, combine oil, onion, garlic, and 3 tablespoons broth. Cook over medium heat, stirring frequently, until onion is tender, about 5 or 6 minutes. If liquid begins to evaporate, add a bit more broth.

Add remaining broth, celery, carrot, green pepper, and tomatoes. Add bay leaf, thyme, chili powder, paprika, salt, if desired, black pepper, and cayenne pepper, if desired. Stir to mix. Bring to a boil. Cover, reduce heat, and simmer 15 minutes.

Return liquid to boiling. Add rice and shrimp. Stir to mix. Cover, reduce heat, and cook 20 minutes or until rice is tender. Remove bay leaf. Stir before serving.

Nutritional Data (based on 8 servings)

PER SERVING		EXCHANGES	
Calories	217	Milk	0.0
Fat (gm)	2.1	Veg.	1.0
Sat. Fat (gm)	0.4	Fruit	0.0
Cholesterol (mg)	87.5	Bread	2.0
Sodium (mg)	217	Meat	1.0
Protein (gm)	14.2	Fat	0.0
Carbohydrate (gm)	34.6		
% Calories from fat	9		

CAJUN FISH

One of the quickest and easiest ways to cook fish is in a non-stick, spray-coated skillet. This tasty variation features fish, along with vegetables in a spicy tomato sauce served over rice.

5-6 Servings

Rice and Vegetables

- 1 cup uncooked long-grain white rice
- 2 teaspoons non-diet, tub-style margarine *or* butter
- 1 cup chopped onion
- 1 garlic clove, minced
- 1 14½-oz. can diced tomatoes, including juice
- 1 large green bell pepper, seeded and chopped
- 2 cups mixed zucchini and yellow squash cubes *or* 2 cups of either
- ½ teaspoon each dried basil leaves and dried thyme leaves
- ¼ teaspoon dried marjoram leaves
- ⅛ teaspoon black pepper
- 2-3 drops hot pepper sauce (optional)
- ¼ teaspoon salt, or to taste (optional)

Fish

- 1 lb. fresh or frozen (thawed) skinless fish fillets, such as flounder, sole, halibut, turbot, or other lean white fish
- ½ teaspoon dried basil leaves
- ¼ teaspoon salt (optional)
- ⅛ teaspoon black pepper

Preheat oven to 200° F.

Rice and Vegetables: Cook rice according to package directions. Set aside.

In large, non-stick skillet, combine margarine, onion, and garlic. Cook over medium heat 6 to 7 minutes or until onion is tender, stirring frequently. Add tomatoes, green pepper, and squash. Add basil, thyme, marjoram, black pepper, and hot pepper sauce, if desired. Stir to combine well. Bring to a boil. Cover, reduce heat, and cook 10 to 15 minutes or until vegetables are tender, stirring occasionally. Add salt, if desired. Remove vegetables to serving platter, and keep warm in oven until fish is cooked.

Fish: Rinse out and dry skillet in which vegetables were cooked. Coat with non-stick cooking spray. Sprinkle basil, salt, if desired, and black pepper evenly over fish.

In batches, if necessary, transfer fish to skillet, and cook over medium heat until cooked through, 2 to 5 minutes per side.

To serve, arrange rice on large serving platter or on individual plates. Top with vegetable mixture, then fish fillets.

Nutritional Data (based on 6 servings)

PER SERVING		EXCHANGES	
Calories	229	Milk	0.0
Fat (gm)	2.7	Veg.	2.0
Sat. Fat (gm)	0.6	Fruit	0.0
Cholesterol (mg)	40	Bread	1.0
Sodium (mg)	206	Meat	2.0
Protein (gm)	18	Fat	0.0
Carbohydrate (gm)	33		
% Calories from fat	11		

SCALLOPS, ITALIAN STYLE

*Scallops make a quick and easy skillet dinner, which
is also wonderfully low in fat.*

4-5 Servings

1¼ cups uncooked long-grain white rice
3 tablespoons defatted chicken broth
2 teaspoons olive oil
1 medium onion, chopped
1 garlic clove, minced
1 medium green bell pepper, seeded and diced
1 14½-oz. can Italian-style tomatoes, including juice
½ cup dry sherry
1 bay leaf
1 teaspoon dried basil leaves
⅛ teaspoon black pepper
2 cups broccoli florets
2 teaspoons cornstarch
¼ cup cold water
¾ lb. bay or ocean scallops
Salt to taste (optional)

Cook rice according to package directions.

In large, non-stick skillet, combine broth, oil, onion, garlic, and green pepper. Cook over medium heat, stirring frequently, until onion is soft, about 5 or 6 minutes. Add tomatoes, breaking them up with large spoon.

Stir in sherry, bay leaf, basil, and black pepper and mix well. Add broccoli florets. Cover and bring to a boil. Lower heat and simmer 4 minutes or until broccoli is partially cooked.

Stir together cornstarch and water. Bring liquid in skillet to a boil. Stir in cornstarch-water mixture, and cook, stirring, until sauce thickens slightly. Cook 1 minute longer.

Stir in scallops. Cover and cook 3 minutes longer or until scallops are cooked through. If desired, add salt.

Serve over white rice.

Nutritional Data (based on 5 servings)

PER SERVING		EXCHANGES	
Calories	339	Milk	0.0
Fat (gm)	3.5	Veg.	2.0
Sat. Fat (gm)	0.4	Fruit	0.0
Cholesterol (mg)	37	Bread	2.5
Sodium (mg)	352	Meat	2.0
Protein (gm)	22	Fat	0.0
Carbohydrate (gm)	50		
% Calories from fat	9		

FLOUNDER FLORENTINE

Here's a fast and flavorful fish dinner. The recipe calls for floun-der, but you can substitute any lean, mild white fish such as sole, halibut, or turbot. The fresh tomato in the recipe makes a nice contrast with the spinach.

4-5 Servings

7-9 ozs. uncooked penne rigate *or* mostaccioli *or* similar pasta shape, preferably ridged
¼ teaspoon salt (optional)
⅛ teaspoon black pepper
1 lb. fresh or frozen (thawed) skinless flounder fillets
2 tablespoons dry sherry
2 teaspoons olive oil
1 medium onion, thinly sliced
1 garlic clove, minced
1 package frozen chopped spinach, thawed and well drained
1 large tomato, cored and cubed
¾ cup defatted chicken broth
1 teaspoon each dried thyme leaves and dried basil leaves
½ teaspoon salt, or to taste (optional)
⅛ teaspoon ground black pepper
1 oz. (¼ cup) grated Parmesan cheese

Cook pasta according to package directions. Rinse and drain in colander.

Meanwhile, spray-coat a large non-stick skillet. Sprinkle salt, if desired, and black pepper evenly over fish.

In batches if necessary, add fish to skillet, and cook over medium heat until cooked through, 2 to 6 minutes per side. Remove fish from skillet and keep warm.

Rinse out and dry skillet in which fish was cooked. In skillet, combine sherry, oil, onion, and garlic. Cook over medium heat 5 or 6 minutes, stirring frequently, until onion is tender. Add spinach, tomato, broth, thyme, basil, salt, if desired, and pepper. Stir to combine well. Bring to a boil. Lower heat and cook, uncovered, 3 to 4 minutes or until liquid has reduced somewhat and spinach is done.

Arrange pasta on serving platter. Top with fish and then the tomato-spinach mixture. Sprinkle Parmesan over all.

Nutritional Data (based on 5 servings)

PER SERVING		EXCHANGES	
Calories	304	Milk	0.0
Fat (gm)	6.1	Veg.	1.0
Sat. Fat (gm)	1.8	Fruit	0.0
Cholesterol (mg)	87	Bread	2.0
Sodium (mg)	288	Meat	2.5
Protein (gm)	28	Fat	0.0
Carbohydrate (gm)	33		
% Calories from fat	18		

SALMON AND CANNELLINI OVER PASTA

Although the combination of ingredients may seem a bit unusual, I got the idea for this delicious recipe during a dinner at one of Washington, D.C.'s most acclaimed Italian restaurants.

5-6 Servings

Salmon

 1 lb. Atlantic salmon fillets or steaks, skin removed and cut into 2-in. pieces
 ½ teaspoon salt (optional)
 ¼ teaspoon black pepper

Beans and Vegetables

 4 plum tomatoes, chopped
 ¼ cup finely chopped green onion
 1 medium-sized green bell pepper, seeded and diced
 1 small garlic clove, minced
 2 teaspoons olive oil
 ¾ cup defatted chicken broth
 2½ cups cooked cannellini beans *or* 1 19-oz. can cannellini beans, rinsed and drained
 ½ teaspoon each dried thyme leaves and dried basil leaves
 ¼ teaspoon dried oregano leaves
 ¼ teaspoon salt, or to taste (optional)
 ⅛ teaspoon black pepper

Pasta and Garnish

10-12 ozs. uncooked linguine *or* spaghetti
 2 teaspoons grated Parmesan cheese per serving (optional)
 Chopped parsley (optional)

Salmon: Sprinkle salmon with salt, if desired, and pepper. In large, non-stick skillet coated with non-stick spray, cook salmon over medium heat until cooked through, about 11 to 12 minutes. Removed from pan and set aside in medium bowl.

Beans and Vegetables: Rinse out and dry pan in which fish was cooked. In pan, combine tomatoes, green onion, green pepper, garlic, and oil. Cook over medium heat, stirring frequently, about 4 to 5 minutes. Add broth, beans, thyme, basil, oregano, salt, if using, and pepper. Bring to a boil. Reduce heat and cook, uncovered, about 8 minutes. Return salmon to pan, and cook an additional 1 or 2 minutes or until sauce has thickened slightly and flavors are blended.

Pasta and Garnish: Meanwhile, cook linguine according to package directions. Rinse and drain well in colander. Serve bean and salmon mixture over pasta. Garnish with Parmesan cheese and chopped parsley, if desired.

Nutritional Data (based on 6 servings)

PER SERVING		EXCHANGES	
Calories	404	Milk	0.0
Fat (gm)	8.6	Veg.	1.0
Sat. Fat (gm)	1.2	Fruit	0.0
Cholesterol (mg)	83	Bread	3.5
Sodium (mg)	95	Meat	2.0
Protein (gm)	28	Fat	0.5
Carbohydrate (gm)	54		
% Calories from fat	19		

GARLIC, SHRIMP, AND VEGETABLE STIR-FRY

Here's a quick and easy shrimp and vegetable dish. Hoisin sauce, used extensively in Chinese cookery, is available at specialty food stores and some supermarkets. So is "hot oil," a spicy oriental seasoning, for which hot pepper sauce can be substituted.

4-5 Servings

1¼ cups uncooked long-grain white rice
2 tablespoons dry sherry
2 tablespoons defatted chicken broth
2 tablespoons reduced-sodium soy sauce
2 teaspoons sesame oil
2 large garlic cloves, minced
2 drops "hot oil"
½ lb. snow peas, stem ends removed
1 red bell pepper, seeded and cut into cubes

¼ cup thinly sliced green onion

1 lb. medium shrimp, uncooked, peeled, and deveined

¼ cup water

2 teaspoons cornstarch

2 tablespoons Hoisin sauce

½ teaspoon lemon juice

Cook rice according to package directions.

In large non-stick skillet, stir together sherry, broth, soy sauce, sesame oil, garlic, and hot oil.

Add snow peas, red pepper, and onion and cook quickly over medium-high heat, stirring, 2 minutes. Add shrimp and simmer, stirring, 4 or 5 minutes longer or until shrimp curls.

In a cup, stir together water and cornstarch. Add to pan and cook, stirring, 1 or 2 minutes or until sauce thickens. Stir in Hoisin sauce and lemon juice.

Serve shrimp and vegetables over rice.

Nutritional Data (based on 5 servings)

PER SERVING		EXCHANGES	
Calories	303	Milk	0.0
Fat (gm)	3.1	Veg.	1.5
Sat. Fat (gm)	0.6	Fruit	0.0
Cholesterol (mg)	139	Bread	2.5
Sodium (mg)	465	Meat	1.5
Protein (gm)	21	Fat	0.0
Carbohydrate (gm)	45		
% Calories from fat	9		

TUNA, PASTA, BROCCOLI CASSEROLE

If you prefer, serve the tuna-broccoli sauce over baked potatoes.

4-5 Servings

3 cups uncooked fusilli *or* other similar pasta shape

3 cups small broccoli florets

1 medium onion, chopped

1 small garlic clove, minced

2 tablespoons defatted chicken broth

1 tablespoon non-diet, tub-style margarine *or* butter

1½ tablespoons white flour

1½ cups 1% fat milk

1 teaspoon lemon juice

½ teaspoon each dried thyme leaves and dried basil leaves

¼ teaspoon dry mustard

⅛ teaspoon white pepper

½ teaspoon salt, or to taste (optional)

1 6½-oz. can water-packed tuna, drained and flaked

2 ozs. grated Parmesan cheese (½ cup)

Preheat oven to 375° F.

In small Dutch oven or similar pot, bring 3 qts. water to a boil. Add fusilli. Cook 8 to 10 minutes. Add broccoli and boil an additional 3 to 4 minutes or until pasta is tender. Drain in colander. Transfer to 3-qt. casserole, reserving a few broccoli florets for garnish.

In medium saucepan, combine onion, garlic, chicken broth, and margarine. Cook over medium heat, stirring frequently, 6 to 7 minutes or until onion is tender.

Stir in flour and stir to make a smooth paste. Gradually add milk, stirring constantly to make sure mixture remains smooth. Add lemon juice, thyme, basil, mustard, pepper, and salt, if using. Stir to mix.

Reduce heat and cook, stirring, until milk has thickened. Reduce heat to low. Cook 1 minute longer, stirring. Stir in tuna and continue to cook an additional 1 or 2 minutes. Stir in cheese.

Stir sauce into pasta-broccoli mixture. Bake 15 to 20 minutes or until casserole is hot. Garnish with reserved broccoli florets.

Nutritional Data (based on 5 servings)

PER SERVING		EXCHANGES	
Calories	414	Milk	0.5
Fat (gm)	8.5	Veg.	1.0
Sat. Fat (gm)	3.3	Fruit	0.0
Cholesterol (mg)	18	Bread	3.0
Sodium (mg)	329	Meat	2.0
Protein (gm)	27	Fat	0.5
Carbohydrate (gm)	59		
% Calories from fat	18		

PINE BARK STEW

I happened upon this wonderfully satisfying fish stew at a restaurant on River Street in Savannah. In this reduced-fat version, some of the ingredients are different, but I think I've recreated the rich and creamy taste and texture of the original.

8-9 Servings

2 teaspoons non-diet, tub-style margarine *or* butter
2 cups chopped onion
1 large garlic clove, minced
2½ cups defatted chicken broth, divided
1 8-oz. bottle clam juice
3½ cups ¾-in. peeled potato cubes (1¼ lbs.)
2 cups coarsely chopped cauliflower
⅓ cup dry sherry
1 bay leaf
2 teaspoons lemon juice
1½ teaspoons dried thyme leaves
1 teaspoon dried basil leaves
¼ teaspoon powdered mustard
¼ teaspoon (scant) white pepper
¾ cup 1% fat milk
½ lb. mild white fish such as flounder, turbot, or haddock, cut into bite-sized pieces
½ lb. medium shrimp, uncooked, peeled, and deveined
½ lb. bay scallops
¼ teaspoon salt, or to taste (optional)

In Dutch oven or similar large pot, combine margarine, onion, garlic, and 3 tablespoons broth. Cook, stirring frequently, until onion is soft, about 5 minutes. If liquid begins to evaporate, add a bit more broth.

Add remaining broth, clam juice, potatoes, cauliflower, sherry, bay leaf, lemon juice, thyme, basil, mustard, and white pepper. Bring mixture to full boil. Cover, lower heat, and simmer 12 to 15 minutes or until vegetables are tender. Remove bay leaf.

Transfer about 3 cups of vegetables and broth from pot to blender container. Cover and blend on high speed until vegetables are pureed. Stir mixture back into stew. Stir in milk.

Add fish, shrimp, and scallops. Simmer an additional 6 or 7 minutes or until seafood is done and fish begins to flake. Add salt, if desired. Stir before serving.

Nutritional Data (based on 9 servings)

PER SERVING		EXCHANGES	
Calories	163	Milk	0.0
Fat (gm)	2.4	Veg.	0.5
Sat. Fat (gm)	0.8	Fruit	0.0
Cholesterol (mg)	68	Bread	1.0
Sodium (mg)	363	Meat	1.5
Protein (gm)	18	Fat	0.0
Carbohydrate (gm)	18		
% Calories from fat	13		

WILDE LAKE FISH CHOWDER

———————◆———————

Wilde Lake is just a short walk from my house. So I decided to name this chowder after the local landmark. Fish blends very nicely with the variety of textures and flavors in the rich, full-bodied broth. Non-fat ricotta lends creamy texture.

5-6 Servings

- 2 teaspoons olive oil
- 1 cup chopped onion
- 1 large garlic clove, minced
- 3 cups defatted chicken broth, divided
- 1 8-oz. bottle clam juice
- 1 large carrot, peeled and diced
- 2½ cups ¾-in. peeled potato cubes (14 ozs.)
- 1½ cups coarsely chopped cauliflower
- ¼ cup dry sherry
- 1 bay leaf
- 1½ teaspoons each dried basil leaves and dried thyme leaves
- ¼ teaspoon powdered mustard
- ¼ teaspoon (scant) white pepper
- 1 tablespoon cornstarch
- ¼ cup cold water
- ½ cup non-fat ricotta cheese
- 1 8-oz. can tomato sauce
- 1 lb. mild white fish such as flounder, turbot, or haddock, cut into bite-sized pieces
- ¼ teaspoon salt, or to taste (optional)

In Dutch oven or similar large pot, combine oil, onion, garlic, and 2 table-spoons broth. Cook, stirring frequently, until onion is soft, about 5 minutes. If liquid begins to evaporate, add a bit more broth.

Add remaining broth, clam juice, carrot, potatoes, cauliflower, sherry, bay leaf, basil, thyme, mustard, and pepper. Stir to mix well. Bring to full boil.

Mix cornstarch with water. Add to broth and stir. Boil 1 or 2 minutes or until liquid thickens slightly. Cover, lower heat, and simmer 12 to 15 minutes, stirring occasionally, until vegetables are tender. Remove bay leaf.

In blender container, combine ricotta cheese and about 2 cups of vegetables and broth from pot. Blend on high speed until vegetables are pureed.

Stir ricotta-vegetable mixture back into soup. Stir in tomato sauce. Add fish. Simmer an additional 4 or 5 minutes or until fish begins to flake. Add salt, if desired. Stir before serving.

Nutritional Data (based on 6 servings)

PER SERVING		EXCHANGES	
Calories	214	Milk	0.0
Fat (gm)	3.3	Veg.	1.5
Sat. Fat (gm)	1	Fruit	0.0
Cholesterol (mg)	48	Bread	1.0
Sodium (mg)	690	Meat	2.0
Protein (gm)	21	Fat	0.0
Carbohydrate (gm)	25		
% Calories from fat	13		

MANHATTAN-STYLE CLAM CHOWDER

Canadian bacon rounds out the flavor of this quick and easy chowder.

5-6 Servings

- 2 teaspoons non-diet, tub-style margarine *or* butter
- 1 large onion, finely chopped
- 1 small clove garlic, minced
- 2 large celery stalks, including leaves, diced
- 1 cup defatted chicken broth, divided
- 2 6½-oz. cans chopped clams, including juice
- 1 medium green bell pepper, seeded and diced
- 2 medium boiling potatoes, peeled and diced (¾ lb.)
- 2 ozs. Canadian bacon, cut into thin strips
- 2 14½-oz. cans reduced-sodium diced tomatoes, including juice, *or* regular diced tomatoes
- 1 cup frozen corn kernels
  Dash cayenne pepper
- 1 bay leaf
- ½ teaspoon dried thyme leaves
- ½ teaspoon dried basil leaves
- ½ teaspoon granulated sugar

¼ teaspoon salt, or to taste (optional)
⅛ teaspoon black pepper

In Dutch oven or similar large pot, melt margarine over medium heat. Add onion, garlic, celery, and 3 tablespoons broth. Cook vegetables, stirring frequently, until onion is tender, about 6 minutes. If liquid begins to evaporate, add a bit more broth.

Drain liquid from clams into small bowl, and reserve clams. Add clam liquid to pot, along with remaining broth, green pepper, potatoes, and Canadian bacon. Bring to a boil. Cover, lower heat, and simmer 10 to 12 minutes or until potatoes are tender, stirring occasionally.

Add reserved clams and all remaining ingredients. Re-cover and bring to a boil. Lower heat and simmer about 5 minutes longer until flavors are well blended. Remove and discard bay leaf.

Nutritional Data (based on 6 servings)

PER SERVING		EXCHANGES	
Calories	142	Milk	0.0
Fat (gm)	2.8	Veg.	2.0
Sat. Fat (gm)	0.6	Fruit	0.0
Cholesterol (mg)	5	Bread	1.0
Sodium (mg)	590	Meat	0.5
Protein (gm)	7	Fat	0.0
Carbohydrate (gm)	25		
% Calories from fat	16		

5

VEGETARIAN AND VEGETABLE MEALS

There were only a few vegetarian dishes in my repertory until my daughter, then 11, informed me she was going to stop eating meat. I didn't know how long the new order was going to last, but I decided I'd better start learning about meatless cookery. It's a good thing I did because more than a decade later, she's still a vegetarian. And I'm still on the lookout for delicious recipes without meat.

Many dishes in this chapter are strictly vegetarian. Some do use chicken broth for flavor and convenience. If you're cooking strictly vegetarian, you can substitute vegetable bouillon with equally good results.

Most of the following recipes—such as Black Bean-Tortilla Bake, Curried Lentil-Spinach Soup, and Linguine with Artichoke, Tomato, and Olive Sauce—feature fresh vegetables and hearty beans and grains, which combine to provide high-quality protein. Almost all are relatively quick and easy to prepare, as well as quite inexpensive.

LINGUINE WITH ARTICHOKE, TOMATO, AND OLIVE SAUCE

Because olives are so high in fat and sodium, I serve them only as a special treat—such as in this simple pasta-vegetable dish, where they taste wonderful combined with the artichoke hearts and tomatoes. Also, because the olives go a long way, the total fat content of the dish isn't really very high. If you prefer, pitted black olives could be substituted in the sauce.

4 Servings

- 10 ozs. uncooked linguine
- 2 teaspoons olive oil
- 1 medium onion, finely chopped
- 1 tablespoon water
- 3 medium fresh tomatoes, peeled, cored, and chopped
- 1 14½-oz. jar water-packed artichoke hearts, drained and cut into ½-in. strips
- 10 large green pimiento-stuffed olives, chopped or very thinly sliced
- 2 tablespoons chopped fresh basil *or* 2 teaspoons dried basil
- 1 teaspoon dried oregano leaves
- ¼ teaspoon black pepper
- 2 tablespoons grated Parmesan cheese

Cook linguine according to package directions. Rinse and drain in colander.

In large, non-stick skillet, combine oil, onion, and water. Cook, stirring frequently, until onion is soft, about 5 or 6 minutes. If liquid begins to evaporate, add a bit more water.

Add tomatoes, artichoke hearts, olives, basil, oregano, and black pepper. Stir to mix well. Cook, uncovered, over medium heat, 6 to 8 minutes or until tomatoes have cooked down somewhat and flavors are well blended.

Serve individual portions of sauce over linguine. Top each serving with ½ teaspoon Parmesan cheese.

Nutritional Data

PER SERVING		EXCHANGES	
Calories	372	Milk	0.0
Fat (gm)	7.1	Veg.	3.5
Sat. Fat (gm)	1.4	Fruit	0.0
Cholesterol (mg)	64	Bread	3.0
Sodium (mg)	376	Meat	0.0
Protein (gm)	16	Fat	1.5
Carbohydrate (gm)	66		
% Calories from fat	16		

SPINACH POLENTA WITH HERBED VEGETABLES

◆

For a wonderfully filling dish, top spinach polenta with this flavorful garbanzo and vegetable sauce. Traditionally, polenta requires almost constant stirring. However, this microwave method makes preparation quick and easy. The recipe was designed using a high-powered microwave (900 w.). If yours has less power, you may need to lengthen cooking time. For smooth-textured polenta, follow stirring directions carefully.

5-6 Servings

Vegetables

 2 teaspoons olive oil
 1 medium onion, chopped
 1 garlic clove, minced
 2 cups cooked garbanzo beans *or* 1 15-oz. can garbanzo beans, well drained
 2 cups diced zucchini *or* yellow squash (or a combination of both)
 1 large carrot, peeled and diced
 1 15-oz. can tomato sauce
 1 large bay leaf
 1½ teaspoons dried thyme leaves
 ½ teaspoon dried basil leaves
    Salt to taste (optional)
 ⅛ teaspoon black pepper
 ½ teaspoon granulated sugar (optional)

Polenta

- 1 cup yellow cornmeal
- 1 tablespoon granulated sugar
- ½ teaspoon salt (scant), or to taste (optional)
- 2½ cups water
- ½ cup 1% fat milk
- 1 medium onion, diced
- 1 10-oz. package frozen chopped spinach, thawed and well drained

To Serve

- 2 teaspoons grated Parmesan cheese per serving (optional)

Vegetables: In large saucepan, combine oil, onion, and garlic. Cook over medium heat 5 or 6 minutes or until onion is tender. Add garbanzos, squash, carrot, tomato sauce, bay leaf, thyme, basil, salt, if desired, and pepper. If tomato sauce seems acid, add sugar. Bring to a boil. Reduce heat, cover, and simmer, stirring occasionally, 15 to 20 minutes or until flavors are well blended and vegetables are tender. Remove and discard bay leaf.

Polenta: Combine cornmeal, sugar, salt, if desired, water, milk, and onion in 2½-qt. microwave-safe casserole. Stir to mix well. Microwave, uncovered, on high power 6 to 7 minutes, stopping and stirring with wire whisk after 2 minutes and 4 minutes. After cooking, stir again with wire whisk until mixture is smooth. Stir in spinach. Cover with casserole lid and microwave an additional 3 to 3½ minutes on high power. Remove from microwave and let stand an additional 3 to 4 minutes.

Serve individual portions of vegetable sauce over polenta. Garnish with Parmesan cheese, if desired.

Nutritional Data (based on 6 servings)

PER SERVING		EXCHANGES	
Calories	285	Milk	0.0
Fat (gm)	4.4	Veg.	2.0
Sat. Fat (gm)	0.5	Fruit	0.0
Cholesterol (mg)	1	Bread	2.5
Sodium (mg)	517	Meat	0.0
Protein (gm)	13	Fat	1.0
Carbohydrate (gm)	52		
% Calories from fat	13		

WILD RICE AND ORZO CASSEROLE WITH ASPARAGUS

Wild rice, asparagus, and Parmesan give this dish its wonderful flavor. Orzo, a rice-shaped pasta, provides a nice color and texture contrast to the dark grain. Generally, wild rice needs to cook for an hour. But some manufacturers have reduced the cooking time by partial processing, so check package directions.

5-6 Servings

⅔ cup uncooked wild rice, rinsed and drained
3½ cups reduced-sodium defatted chicken broth
    or regular defatted chicken broth
1 medium onion, chopped
1 garlic clove, minced
1 teaspoon dried thyme leaves
1 teaspoon dried marjoram leaves
¼ teaspoon black pepper
½ cup uncooked orzo
10 medium-sized asparagus spears, trimmed and cut into 1-in. lengths
¾ cup non-fat ricotta cheese
2 ozs. (½ cup) freshly grated Parmesan cheese, divided
    Chopped red bell pepper or additional asparagus tips for garnish (optional)

In large saucepan or small pot, combine rice, broth, onion, garlic, thyme, marjoram, and pepper. Bring to full boil. Cover, reduce heat, and cook 1 hour (or according to package directions), reducing heat as rice absorbs broth.

Twenty minutes before rice is done, in separate pot, cook orzo according to package directions, adding asparagus to pot during last 3 minutes of cooking time. Transfer orzo, asparagus, and rice to colander and drain.

Preheat oven to 350° F. Transfer rice, asparagus, and orzo mixture to 2-qt. casserole. Stir in ricotta. Stir in all but 2 tablespoons of Parmesan.

At this point, the casserole can be refrigerated up to 24 hours.

Sprinkle casserole top with remaining Parmesan. Bake, covered, 25 to 30 minutes or until heated through. Cooking time will be longer if casserole has been refrigerated. Garnish with chopped red pepper or additional asparagus tips, if desired.

Nutritional Data (based on 6 servings)

PER SERVING		EXCHANGES	
Calories	230	Milk	0.0
Fat (gm)	3.5	Veg.	1.0
Sat. Fat (gm)	1.9	Fruit	0.0
Cholesterol (mg)	7.5	Bread	2.0
Sodium (mg)	391	Meat	1.0
Protein (gm)	16.9	Fat	0.0
Carbohydrate (gm)	34.5		
% Calories from fat	13		

MUSHROOMS FLORENTINE

Here's a pleasing medley of mushrooms, spinach, and Parmesan stirred together in a creamy sauce and mixed with pasta.

4-5 Servings

Pasta

10 ozs. uncooked penne rigate, *or* mostaccioli *or* similar pasta shape, preferably ridged

Sauce

¾ lb. (4½ cups) fresh mushrooms, sliced (preferably large)

1 medium onion, chopped

1 small garlic clove, minced

¼ cup defatted chicken broth

2 teaspoons non-diet, tub-style margarine *or* butter

2 tablespoons white flour

2¼ cups 1% fat milk, divided

¼ cup dry sherry

2 teaspoons lemon juice

2 teaspoons Italian seasoning

½ teaspoon dry mustard

½ teaspoon salt (optional)

¼ teaspoon white pepper

1 10-oz. package frozen chopped spinach,
   thawed and well drained
2 ozs. (½ cup) grated Parmesan cheese

Garnish

Red bell pepper strips (optional)

Pasta: Cook pasta according to package directions. Rinse and drain well in colander. Set aside.

Sauce: In large non-stick skillet, combine mushrooms, onion, garlic, broth, and margarine. Cook over medium heat, stirring frequently, 6 or 7 minutes or until onion is very tender.

Add flour to skillet, and stir to make a smooth paste. Gradually add 1¾ cups milk, stirring constantly to make sure mixture remains smooth. Simmer 4 or 5 minutes longer, stirring frequently, until sauce thickens.

Stir in remaining milk, sherry, lemon juice, Italian seasoning, mustard, salt, if desired, and pepper. Stir in spinach and cook an additional 3 or 4 minutes. Stir in Parmesan cheese.

Transfer pasta to 3-qt. casserole. Stir in sauce.

Garnish with sweet red pepper, if desired.

Nutritional Data (based on 5 servings)

PER SERVING		EXCHANGES	
Calories	378	Milk	0.5
Fat (gm)	8.4	Veg.	2.0
Sat. Fat (gm)	3.5	Fruit	0.0
Cholesterol (mg)	62	Bread	3.0
Sodium (mg)	366	Meat	0.0
Protein (gm)	21	Fat	1.5
Carbohydrate (gm)	56		
% Calories from fat	20		

MIXED GRAINS AND BEAN CASSEROLE CON QUESO

◆

*I love the variety of colors and textures in this delicious casserole.
All the grains are cooked in one pot. But because they vary
greatly in the cooking time needed, they're added sequentially.
Incidentally, the recipe uses wild rice that cooks in 45 minutes.
If you have a brand that needs a slightly longer cooking time,
adjust accordingly. Also, make sure water returns to
boiling after each addition of grain.*

6-7 Servings

1   medium onion, chopped
2   garlic cloves, minced
½   cup uncooked wild rice, rinsed and drained
2   large bay leaves
⅔   cup uncooked orzo
1   cup frozen corn kernels
⅓   cup uncooked couscous
2   cups cooked kidney beans *or* 1 15-oz. can
    kidney beans, washed and drained
1   cup 1% fat cottage cheese
1   4-oz. can chopped green chilies, drained
1½ teaspoons chili powder
½   teaspoon salt, or to taste (optional)
⅛   teaspoon black pepper, or to taste
8   ozs. (2 cups) grated reduced-fat sharp
    Cheddar cheese
    Parsley sprigs or chopped chives for garnish
    (optional)

In large, heavy pot, bring 3 quarts of water to a boil. Add onion, garlic, wild
rice, and bay leaves. Cover, reduce heat slightly, and boil 30 minutes. Add
orzo, re-cover, and boil an additional 10 minutes. Add corn. Re-cover and
boil an additional 3 minutes. Add couscous. Re-cover and cook an additional 2 minutes. Remove pot from burner, and allow to stand 5 minutes.

Preheat oven to 375° F.

Drain grains in colander. Remove bay leaves and discard. Transfer to 3-qt.,
oven-proof casserole. Stir in kidney beans, cottage cheese, and chilies. Stir

in chili powder, salt, if desired, and pepper. Gently stir in Cheddar cheese. Bake, covered, until heated through, 30 to 35 minutes.

Garnish with parsley sprigs or chopped chives, if desired.

Nutritional Data (based on 7 servings)

PER SERVING		EXCHANGES	
Calories	357	Milk	0.0
Fat (gm)	5.9	Veg.	1.0
Sat. Fat (gm)	2.7	Fruit	0.0
Cholesterol (mg)	18.8	Bread	3.0
Sodium (mg)	641	Meat	2.0
Protein (gm)	22	Fat	0.0
Carbohydrate (gm)	54.3		
% Calories from fat	15		

BAKED BURRITO CASSEROLE

Here's a tasty, hearty burrito casserole that is quite low in fat. It's also very quick and easy to assemble. The recipe calls for pinto beans. If they are unavailable, kidney beans can be used. The casserole can be cooked either in the oven or the microwave. To get just the amount of "heat" I like in the picante sauce, I usually mix mild and medium together.

5 Servings

Filling

4 cups cooked pinto beans *or* 2 15-oz. cans pinto beans, drained

1 8-oz. can reduced-sodium tomato sauce *or* regular tomato sauce

½ cup mild or medium picante sauce

1 teaspoon chili powder

3 ozs. (¾ cup) grated reduced-fat sharp Cheddar cheese

3 ozs. (¾ cup) grated non-fat Cheddar cheese food *or* non-fat mozzarella

Tortillas and Topping

10 6-in. flour tortillas

⅔ cup mild or medium picante sauce

½ cup non-fat sour cream

Spray 2-qt. flat, rectangular baking dish with non-stick spray and set aside.

Filling: In food processor container, combine beans, tomato sauce, picante sauce, and chili powder. Process just until beans are partially pureed.

Combine the 2 cheeses and reserve.

Tortillas and Topping: For each burrito, lay a tortilla flat and spoon ⅓ cup of bean mixture in a line down its center. Sprinkle with 2 tablespoons of cheese mixture. Carefully roll up each tortilla, and lay them side by side, seam side down, in sprayed baking dish. Press burritos together as dish fills and make sure top surfaces are smooth.

Conventional Method: Preheat oven to 375° F. Bake, uncovered, 11 to 14 minutes or until cheese is melted and tortillas begin to crisp at edges.

Remove from oven. Spoon picante sauce in double line down length of tortillas, leaving about 2 inches between lines. Bake 2 minutes longer.

Microwave Method: Cover baking dish with wax paper. Microwave on high power 6 to 7 minutes or until cheese is melted and filling is hot, turning dish one-quarter turn twice during microwaving. Remove from microwave. Spoon picante sauce in double line down length of tortillas, leaving about 2 inches between lines. Recover with fresh wax paper, and microwave an additional 45 to 90 seconds.

To Complete Casserole: Remove baking dish from oven or microwave. Spoon a line of sour cream down length of burritos.

Leftover casserole can easily be rewarmed in the microwave.

Nutritional Data

PER SERVING		EXCHANGES	
Calories	509	Milk	0.0
Fat (gm)	8.3	Veg.	1.0
Sat. Fat (gm)	3.1	Fruit	0.0
Cholesterol (mg)	10	Bread	5.0
Sodium (mg)	778	Meat	2.0
Protein (gm)	29	Fat	1.0
Carbohydrate (gm)	82		
% Calories from fat	15		

BLACK BEAN-TORTILLA BAKE

This Tex-Mex casserole is put together like lasagna. However, the filling is a spicy black bean mixture alternated with tortillas instead of pasta. The recipe calls for either mild or medium picante sauce. To get the degree of "heat" I like, I generally use a combination of the two.

8 Servings

1 cup shredded reduced-fat Cheddar cheese (4 ozs.)
1 cup shredded non-fat Cheddar cheese (4 ozs.)
1 large onion, chopped
2 garlic cloves, minced
2 teaspoons olive oil
3 tablespoons water
1 large green bell pepper, seeded and chopped
1 cup mild *or* medium picante sauce
1 15-oz. can tomato sauce
1½ teaspoons ground cumin
1 teaspoon chili powder
4 cups cooked black beans *or* 2 15-oz. cans black beans, rinsed and well drained
16 6-in. corn tortillas
1 cup non-fat ricotta cheese
1 large tomato, chopped, for garnish
½ cup non-fat sour cream, for garnish

Preheat oven to 350° F.

Mix Cheddar cheeses together in medium bowl and set aside.

In small pot or very large saucepan, combine onion, garlic, oil, and water. Cook over medium heat, stirring frequently, until onion is soft, about 5 or 6 minutes. If liquid begins to evaporate, add a bit more water. Add green pepper, picante sauce, tomato sauce, cumin, and chili powder. Simmer, uncovered, 5 minutes. Stir in beans. Remove from burner.

Spread ½ of bean mixture evenly in bottom of 9½ x 13-inch baking pan. Top with 8 tortillas in overlapping layer. With back of large spoon, spread non-fat ricotta evenly over tortillas. Top with ½ of Cheddar cheese mixture. Add remaining tortillas, then remaining bean mixture.

Cover with aluminum foil and bake 30 to 35 minutes or until heated through. Sprinkle with remaining Cheddar cheese mixture, and bake, uncovered, an additional 5 to 6 minutes or until cheese is partially melted.

To serve, cut into 8 rectangles and garnish with tomatoes and sour cream.

Nutritional Data

PER SERVING		EXCHANGES	
Calories	382	Milk	0.0
Fat (gm)	7.1	Veg.	0.5
Sat. Fat (gm)	2.5	Fruit	0.0
Cholesterol (mg)	14	Bread	3.0
Sodium (mg)	723	Meat	3.0
Protein (gm)	27	Fat	0.0
Carbohydrate (gm)	59		
% Calories from fat	16		

STIR-FRIED TOFU, VEGETABLES, AND RICE NOODLES

Rice sticks (actually rice noodles) are great for oriental dishes because they cook so quickly—and absorb the flavor of the sauce with which they're mixed. They, the "hot oil," and the fermented black beans featured in this recipe are available at specialty markets and the oriental section of large grocery stores.

4 Servings

3½ ozs. uncooked rice sticks
2 tablespoons reduced-sodium soy sauce
2 tablespoons dry sherry
2-3 drops "hot oil"
1 10½-oz. package firm tofu, cut into small cubes
1 tablespoon sesame oil
¼ cup sliced green onion tops
1 clove garlic, minced
½ tablespoon fermented black beans
1 large celery stalk, sliced diagonally
3 cups sliced bok choy stems and leaves
½ cup vegetable broth *or* defatted chicken broth

½ large red bell pepper, seeded and diced
1 14-oz. can baby corn, well drained

Soak rice sticks in hot water for 10 minutes.

Meanwhile, in medium bowl, combine soy sauce, sherry, and hot oil. Stir to mix well. Add tofu and stir to coat. Marinate at room temperature 10 minutes, stirring occasionally.

Drain rice sticks in colander. Cut into 2-inch lengths and reserve.

Place sesame oil in large non-stick skillet. With slotted spoon, transfer tofu from marinade to skillet. Reserve marinade. Cook tofu over medium heat, stirring frequently, 2 or 3 minutes. Add onion, garlic, black beans, and celery. Cook an additional 2 or 3 minutes. Add onion, garlic, black beans, and celery. Cook an additional 2 or 3 minutes, stirring frequently.

Add bok choy, reserved marinade, and broth and cook an additional 7 minutes. Add red pepper, corn, and reserved rice noodles and stir to mix well. Cook an additional 2 or 3 minutes to heat vegetables.

Nutritional Data

PER SERVING		EXCHANGES	
Calories	338	Milk	0.0
Fat (gm)	10.3	Veg.	1.0
Sat. Fat (gm)	1.4	Fruit	0.0
Cholesterol (mg)	0.0	Bread	2.5
Sodium (mg)	342	Meat	1.5
Protein (gm)	17	Fat	1.0
Carbohydrate (gm)	48		
% Calories from fat	25		

SOUTH OF THE BORDER POTATO, BEAN, AND CHEESE SOUP

I love cheese, but when I first got serious about low-fat cooking, I thought I had to cut this food completely out of my diet. Then I began experimenting with recipes like this one and my Taco Salad (see p. 141), in which salsa and other spicy ingredients intensify the flavor of reduced-fat Cheddar. Try this satisfying soup, and you'll discover what I mean.

6-7 Servings

2 teaspoons olive oil
1 cup chopped onion
1 garlic clove, minced
4 cups defatted chicken broth, divided
1½ cups 1% fat milk
5 cups peeled and cubed (½ in.) boiling potatoes
¼ teaspoon black pepper
1 teaspoon chili powder
1¼ cups (5 ozs.) shredded reduced-fat Cheddar cheese
4 cups cooked kidney beans *or* 2 16-oz. cans kidney beans, well drained
1½ cups mild, reduced-sodium salsa *or* regular salsa

In large pot, combine oil, onion, garlic, and 2 tablespoons broth. Cook over medium heat, stirring frequently, about 5 minutes or until onion is tender. If liquid begins to evaporate, add a bit more broth.

Add remaining broth, milk, potatoes, and pepper. Bring to a boil. Lower heat and simmer, covered, 12 to 14 minutes or until potatoes are tender, stirring occasionally. Remove pot from burner.

Using ladle, transfer about half of vegetables and liquid from pot to blender container. Blend on medium speed until thoroughly pureed. Return puree to pot.

Add chili powder. Stir in cheese until melted. Stir in beans and salsa. Cook over low heat an additional 3 or 4 minutes, but do not boil.

Nutritional Data (based on 7 servings)

PER SERVING		EXCHANGES	
Calories	394	Milk	0.0
Fat (gm)	6.8	Veg.	1.0
Sat. Fat (gm)	3.4	Fruit	0.0
Cholesterol (mg)	23	Bread	3.5
Sodium (mg)	793	Meat	2.0
Protein (gm)	21	Fat	0.5
Carbohydrate (gm)	64		
% Calories from fat	15		

CURRIED LENTIL-SPINACH SOUP

Lentils and spinach blend nicely to lend flavor and texture to this vegetarian soup, which is very low in fat. If you like, substitute chicken broth for the vegetable bouillon.

6-7 Servings

- 2 teaspoons olive oil
- 2 cups chopped onion
- 2 large garlic cloves, minced
- 5 cups reduced-sodium vegetable broth *or* defatted chicken broth, divided
- 2 cups water
- 1 celery stalk, thinly sliced
- 1 large carrot, peeled and thinly sliced
- 1 cup brown lentils, rinsed and drained
- 2-2½ teaspoons mild curry powder, or to taste
- ½ teaspoon chili powder
- ¼ teaspoon black pepper
- 1 10-oz. package frozen chopped spinach, thawed and well drained
- 1 14½-oz. can reduced-sodium tomatoes *or* regular tomatoes, including juice, chopped
  Salt to taste (optional)

In large pot, combine oil, onion, garlic, and 3 tablespoons bouillon. Cook over medium heat, stirring frequently, until onion is tender, about 5 or 6 minutes. Add remaining bouillon, along with water, celery, carrot, lentils, curry powder, chili powder, and pepper. Bring to a boil. Lower heat and simmer, covered, about 45 minutes.

Add spinach, tomatoes, and salt, if desired. Simmer an additional 10 minutes until flavors are well blended.

Nutritional Data (based on 7 servings)

PER SERVING		EXCHANGES	
Calories	181	Milk	0.0
Fat (gm)	2	Veg.	2.0
Sat. Fat (gm)	0.3	Fruit	0.0
Cholesterol (mg)	0	Bread	1.5
Sodium (mg)	104	Meat	0.5
Protein (gm)	10.5	Fat	0.0
Carbohydrate (gm)	32.6		
% Calories from fat	10		

6
SLOW-COOKER MEALS

T he recipes in this chapter are designed especially for no-fuss, slow cookery. Many are almost as simple as combining all the ingredients in your slow cooker and just turning it on. There's a wide selection of recipes from which to choose, including Chunky Chicken Soup, Texas Barbecued Beef and Beans, and a German-Style Dinner.

Most are designed for a large Crock-Pot—one that holds 5 quarts. If you're new to slow cookery, buy one with a removable liner, which makes cleanup easy. Also be sure to read the directions that come with the appliance before proceeding.

In general, slow-cooked dishes need less liquid than conventionally prepared recipes because the low cooking temperature and tight-fitting lid make for little or no evaporation. Also, meat tends to cook more quickly than vegetables, so carrots, celery, potatoes, and onion should be diced or cut into small pieces and placed at the bottom of the pot where they get the most heat. (When you plan to start a slow-cooking dish in the morning but know you're going to be in a hurry, you may want to dice the vegetables the night before and refrigerate them.)

I've also found that slow cookery changes the tastes of some foods. A number of seasonings such as bay are intensified so you may want to use less than in a conventional recipe. Seasonings such as onion and chili powder actually become more mellow so you may need more than usual.

Usually it isn't necessary to brown meat before putting it into the slow cooker. The one exception is ground beef, which looks more attractive if browned first using conventional methods.

Most slow cookers have only two temperatures: high and low. But within these settings, there can be some variation in cooking times. That's one reason why the cooking directions are fairly flexible in the recipes that follow.

Another point to remember is that lifting the lid during cooking will significantly lengthen the time needed. Therefore, it's a good idea to leave the pot undisturbed except when additional ingredients are added. If you want to peek at the food, shake the droplets of water off the inside of the lid without removing it.

It's best to start dishes on high to raise meat to a safe temperature more quickly. But if you don't have time to cook the food on high for an hour, you can bring the ingredients to a boil in a conventional pot on the stove and transfer them to the slow cooker. Then set the temperature to low, and proceed with the recipe as directed.

Also, it rarely hurts to continue cooking a dish an hour or two after the ingredients are tender if that turns out to be most convenient.

Usually, two hours of cooking on low equal one hour of cooking on high. So although the recipes in this chapter call for most of the cooking at the low setting, you can almost always halve the cooking time by simply shifting to high.

SLOW-COOKER STEW

---

*Here's a robust beef stew that includes both
potatoes and rice. The potatoes add chunky texture.
The rice helps thicken the flavorful sauce.*

5-6 Servings

- 1 large onion, finely chopped
- 2 garlic cloves, minced
- 1 lb. boiling potatoes, peeled or unpeeled, and cut into ¾-in. cubes (about 3½ cups)
- 1½ cups coarsely shredded cabbage
- 1 large carrot, peeled and sliced
- ¼ cup uncooked long-grain white rice
- 1 lb. beef round, trimmed of all fat and cut into small bite-sized pieces
- 1½ cups defatted beef broth *or* bouillon
- ¾ cup red wine
- ¼ cup ketchup
- 2 teaspoons packed light brown sugar
- ½ tablespoon apple cider vinegar
- 1½ teaspoons dried thyme leaves
- 1 teaspoon chili powder
- ½ teaspoon powdered mustard
- ¼ teaspoon black pepper

In large slow cooker, combine onion, garlic, potatoes, cabbage, carrot, and rice. Add meat. In 4-cup measure or similar bowl, stir together broth, wine, ketchup, brown sugar, vinegar, thyme, chili powder, mustard, and black pepper. Pour mixture over meat and vegetables. Cover pot and cook 1 hour on high. Stir meat and vegetables into sauce, and cook an additional 6½ to 8 hours on low.

Nutritional Data (based on 6 servings)

PER SERVING		EXCHANGES	
Calories	289	Milk	0.0
Fat (gm)	6.0	Veg.	1.5
Sat. Fat (gm)	1.9	Fruit	0.0
Cholesterol (mg)	51	Bread	1.5
Sodium (mg)	287	Meat	2.5
Protein (gm)	21	Fat	0.0
Carbohydrate (gm)	34		
% Calories from fat	18		

TEXAS BARBECUED BEEF AND BEANS

If you love a meal that's both easy and spicy, this barbecued beef and bean dinner is for you.

6-7 Servings

1½ cups finely chopped onion
1 8-oz. can tomato sauce
½ cup mild or medium salsa
2 tablespoons cider vinegar
1½ tablespoons brown sugar
1 tablespoon chili powder
2 teaspoons Worcestershire sauce
¼ teaspoon black pepper
1 lb. beef round, trimmed of all fat and cut into narrow strips
2 garlic cloves, minced
6 cups cooked kidney beans *or* 3 16-oz. cans kidney beans, well drained

In large slow-cooker, stir together onion, tomato sauce, salsa, vinegar, brown sugar, chili powder, Worcestershire sauce, and pepper. Stir in beef, garlic, and beans. Cover and cook on high 1 hour. Lower heat and cook on low 5 to 6 hours or until flavors are well blended.

Nutritional Data (based on 7 servings)

PER SERVING		EXCHANGES	
Calories	363	Milk	0.0
Fat (gm)	5.8	Veg.	1.0
Sat. Fat (gm)	1.8	Fruit	0.0
Cholesterol (mg)	63	Bread	2.5
Sodium (mg)	398	Meat	3.0
Protein (gm)	35	Fat	0.0
Carbohydrate (gm)	44		
% Calories from fat	14		

GROUND BEEF, RICE, AND CABBAGE HOT POT

For firm rice texture, don't overcook this full-bodied beef, cabbage, and rice combo.

6-7 Servings

1 lb. ground round of beef
2 cups finely chopped onion
2 garlic cloves, minced
6 cups reduced-sodium defatted chicken broth *or* regular defatted chicken broth
½ cup ketchup
3 cups finely shredded cabbage, coarse ribs excluded
1 cup uncooked long-grain white rice
1½ cups frozen corn kernels
1 large carrot, peeled and sliced
2 teaspoons dried thyme leaves
1 teaspoon granulated sugar
1 bay leaf
¼ teaspoon ground cinnamon
¼ teaspoon black pepper
Salt to taste (optional)

In large skillet, combine ground round, onion, and garlic. Cook over medium heat, stirring frequently, until beef has changed color.

Turn out meat mixture onto large plate lined with paper towels to absorb any excess fat.

Transfer meat mixture to slow cooker. Add all remaining ingredients except salt. Stir to mix well.

Cover and cook on low setting 5½ to 6 hours or until rice is cooked and flavors are well blended. Remove and discard bay leaf. Add salt, if desired.

Nutritional Data (based on 7 servings)

PER SERVING		EXCHANGES	
Calories	324	Milk	0.0
Fat (gm)	9.3	Veg.	1.5
Sat. Fat (gm)	3.2	Fruit	0.0
Cholesterol (mg)	40	Bread	2.0
Sodium (mg)	568	Meat	2.0
Protein (gm)	21	Fat	0.5
Carbohydrate (gm)	43		
% Calories from fat	25		

BLIZZARD CHILI

During the great East Coast blizzard of 1993, I was looking forward to being snowed in with a large recipe of chili simmering in the Crock-Pot. When I started to assemble the ingredients, however, I found that I did not have enough of a vital component, kidney beans. Making some quick substitutions, I saved my pot of chili—and came up with a nice variation on a favorite theme.

5-6 Servings

- 1 lb. ground round of beef
- 2 cups finely chopped onion
- 1 garlic clove
- 2 cups cooked kidney beans *or* 1 16-oz. can kidney beans, drained
- 2 cups cooked black beans *or* 1 16-oz. can black beans, well drained
- 2½ cups cooked white kidney beans *or* 1 19-oz. can canolini beans, well drained
- 2 15-oz. cans reduced-sodium tomato sauce *or* regular tomato sauce
- 1 bay leaf
- 1 tablespoon chili powder
- 2 teaspoons granulated sugar
- 1 teaspoon ground cumin
- ⅛ teaspoon black pepper
- Salt to taste (optional)

In large skillet, combine ground beef, onion, and garlic. Cook over medium heat, stirring frequently, until beef has changed color.

Turn out meat mixture onto large plate lined with paper towels to absorb any excess fat.

Transfer meat mixture to a slow cooker. Add all remaining ingredients except salt. Stir to mix well.

Cover and cook on low 4 to 5½ hours or until flavors are well blended. Add salt to taste, if desired.

Nutritional Data (based on 6 servings)

PER SERVING		EXCHANGES	
Calories	457	Milk	0.0
Fat (gm)	10.4	Veg.	3.0
Sat. Fat (gm)	3.8	Fruit	0.0
Cholesterol (mg)	47	Bread	2.5
Sodium (mg)	98	Meat	3.0
Protein (gm)	33	Fat	0.5
Carbohydrate (gm)	59		
% Calories from fat	20		

GERMAN-STYLE DINNER

This is the perfect combination of ingredients for a delicious, Old-World dinner. While sauerkraut is a bit high in sodium, a flavorful dish like this makes an occasional indulgence worthwhile.

5-6 Servings

- 2 cups fresh sauerkraut
- 2 large apples, cored and thinly sliced
- 1 large onion, finely chopped
- 2 cups thinly sliced, peeled potatoes
- 1½ cups peeled rutabaga cubes
- 6 ozs. reduced-sodium ham steak *or* regular ham steak, cut into small pieces
- 2 bay leaves
- ⅛ teaspoon black pepper
- ¾ cup cranberry juice cocktail *or* apple cider
- 1½ tablespoons packed light brown sugar

In large slow cooker, combine sauerkraut, apples, onion, potatoes, rutabaga, and ham. Add bay leaves and pepper. In small bowl, mix together cranberry juice and brown sugar. Pour over sauerkraut mixture.

Cover and cook on high heat 1 hour. Stir mixture. Reduce heat to low, and cook an additional 6 to 7 hours.

Nutritional Data (based on 6 servings)

PER SERVING		EXCHANGES	
Calories	242	Milk	0.0
Fat (gm)	1.6	Veg.	1.5
Sat. Fat (gm)	0.1	Fruit	1.5
Cholesterol (mg)	0.0	Bread	1.5
Sodium (mg)	684	Meat	0.0
Protein (gm)	5	Fat	0.0
Carbohydrate (gm)	55		
% Calories from fat	6		

HOPPIN' JOHN

Hoppin' John is a tasty Carolina dish featuring black-eyed peas and rice, which dates back to colonial days. This very modern version is made in a Crock-Pot.

5-6 Servings

- 2 10-oz. packages frozen black-eyed peas, thawed
- 1 large onion, chopped
- 2 cloves garlic, minced
- 1 green pepper, seeded and chopped
- 1 large carrot, peeled and chopped
- 1 14½-oz. can reduced-sodium stewed tomatoes *or* regular stewed tomatoes
- 2½ cups defatted chicken broth
- 8 ozs. ham steak, trimmed of all fat and diced
- 2 teaspoons dried thyme leaves
- ½ teaspoon dry mustard
- ⅛ teaspoon celery salt
- 2 bay leaves
- ¼ teaspoon black pepper
- 2-3 drops Tabasco sauce (optional)
- ¾ cup uncooked long-grain brown rice
  Salt to taste (optional)

Combine all ingredients except rice and salt in large Crock-Pot. Stir to mix well. Cover and cook on high 1 hour. Add rice and stir to mix well. Reduce heat and cook on low 7 to 8 hours until rice is done and flavors are well blended. Remove and discard bay leaves. Stir. Add salt, if desired.

Nutritional Data (based on 6 servings)

PER SERVING		EXCHANGES	
Calories	297	Milk	0.0
Fat (gm)	3.1	Veg.	2.0
Sat. Fat (gm)	0.4	Fruit	0.0
Cholesterol (mg)	0	Bread	3.0
Sodium (mg)	403	Meat	0.5
Protein (gm)	15.7	Fat	0.0
Carbohydrate (gm)	53.1		
% Calories from fat	9		

PORK LOIN WITH POTATO AND CABBAGE

Grated potatoes thicken the sauce in this robust pork stew.

4-5 Servings

1 lb. boiling potatoes (about 3 medium), peeled and grated or shredded

1 14½-oz. can reduced-sodium stewed tomatoes *or* regular stewed tomatoes, including juice

3 cups thinly sliced cabbage, coarse ribs excluded

1 large onion, finely chopped

2 garlic cloves, minced

1 tablespoon packed light brown sugar

2 teaspoons balsamic vinegar

2 teaspoons dried thyme leaves

1 large bay leaf

¼ teaspoon salt, or to taste (optional)

¼ teaspoon black pepper

½ lb. sliced pork loin, trimmed of all fat

1 15-oz. can reduced-sodium tomato sauce *or* regular tomato sauce, divided

In large slow cooker, combine potatoes, tomatoes, cabbage, onion, garlic, brown sugar, vinegar, thyme, bay leaf, salt, if desired, and pepper. Stir to mix well. Add pork slices on top of vegetables. Pour one-half of tomato sauce over all. Reserve remaining tomato sauce in non-reactive container in refrigerator.

Cover pork mixture, and cook on high setting 1 hour. Stir. Reduce heat to low, and cook an additional 5 to 6 hours. Stir in remaining tomato sauce, and cook an additional 5 to 10 minutes.

Nutritional Data (based on 5 servings)

PER SERVING		EXCHANGES	
Calories	249	Milk	0.0
Fat (gm)	2.4	Veg.	4.0
Sat. Fat (gm)	0.7	Fruit	0.0
Cholesterol (mg)	32	Bread	1.0
Sodium (mg)	86	Meat	1.5
Protein (gm)	16	Fat	0.0
Carbohydrate (gm)	43		
% Calories from fat	8		

BAKED BEANS WITH BACON

◆

Vegetarian beans are much lower in fat than baked beans with pork, which is why I use them in this flavorful beans and bacon recipe. Incidentally, adding rice to the recipe not only thickens the sauce but also complements the protein in the beans.

5-6 Servings

1 large onion, finely chopped
1 garlic clove, minced
4 16-oz. cans reduced-sodium vegetarian beans, including sauce, *or* regular vegetarian beans
⅔ cup ketchup
½ cup uncooked long-grain white rice
1 6-oz. package Canadian bacon, cut into thin strips
2 tablespoons light molasses
1 tablespoon packed light brown sugar
1½ tablespoons apple cider vinegar
1 teaspoon powdered mustard
1 teaspoon dried thyme leaves
¼ teaspoon ground cloves
⅛ teaspoon ground ginger

Combine all ingredients in large slow cooker. Cover and cook on high 1 hour. Stir mixture. Turn heat to low and cook an additional 6 to 7 hours or until flavors are well blended.

Nutritional Data (based on 6 servings)

PER SERVING		EXCHANGES	
Calories	465	Milk	0.0
Fat (gm)	4.1	Veg.	1.0
Sat. Fat (gm)	0.9	Fruit	0.0
Cholesterol (mg)	0.0	Bread	4.0
Sodium (mg)	827	Meat	3.0
Protein (gm)	28	Fat	0.0
Carbohydrate (gm)	83		
% Calories from fat	8		

PACIFIC RIM CHICKEN

The combination of sauce ingredients gives this chicken dish a wonderful flavor. Be sure to use large chicken breast halves, as small ones will cook too quickly.

5-6 Servings

1 large onion, finely chopped
1 large green bell pepper, chopped
4-5 large bone-in chicken breast halves, skin and fat removed (about 3½ lbs.)
1 8-oz. can crushed pineapple, including juice
¾ cup defatted reduced-sodium chicken broth *or* regular defatted chicken broth
¼ cup dry sherry
2 tablespoons reduced-sodium soy sauce
1 tablespoon packed light brown sugar
2 teaspoons rice vinegar
½ teaspoon ground ginger
½ teaspoon salt (optional)
¼ teaspoon black pepper
1⅓ cups uncooked long-grain white rice, cooked according to package directions

In large slow cooker, combine onion and green pepper. Arrange chicken over vegetables.

In medium bowl combine pineapple and juice, broth, sherry, soy sauce, brown sugar, vinegar, ginger, salt, if desired, and black pepper. Stir to mix. Pour over chicken.

Cover and cook on high 1 hour. Reduce heat to low, stir chicken into sauce, and cook an additional 5 to 6 hours or until chicken is done.

Remove and reserve chicken in medium bowl. Transfer liquid and vegetables to saucepan. Quickly boil down sauce, stirring frequently, to thicken slightly.

Meanwhile, slice chicken meat. Arrange rice on serving platter. Arrange chicken slices over rice. Pour sauce over all.

Nutritional Data (based on 6 servings)

PER SERVING		EXCHANGES	
Calories	421	Milk	0.0
Fat (gm)	4.9	Veg.	0.5
Sat. Fat (gm)	1.4	Fruit	0.5
Cholesterol (mg)	107	Bread	2.0
Sodium (mg)	277	Meat	4.5
Protein (gm)	43	Fat	0.0
Carbohydrate (gm)	45		
% Calories from fat	11		

CHICKEN WITH FRUIT

Apples, cranberry sauce, and raisins blend with vinegar to make a wonderfully sweet and tangy sauce for chicken. Be sure to use large breast halves, as smaller pieces will cook too quickly.

4-5 Servings

Chicken and Fruit

- 1 cup chopped onion
- 2 tart apples, peeled, cored, and thinly sliced
- 1 cup jellied cranberry sauce
- ½ cup dark raisins
- 1 tablespoon apple cider vinegar
- 1 tablespoon packed brown sugar
- 2-3 large bone-in chicken breast halves, skins removed (about 2½ lbs.)
- ¼ teaspoon salt (optional)
- 1 teaspoon dried thyme leaves
- ¼ teaspoon black pepper

To Serve

- 10 ozs. uncooked reduced-fat egg noodles

Chicken and Fruit: In bottom of large slow cooker, combine onion, apples, cranberry sauce, raisins, vinegar, and brown sugar. Stir to mix well. Sprinkle chicken with salt, if desired, thyme, and pepper. Add to pot on top of fruit mixture. Cover and cook on high 1 hour. Stir chicken into sauce. Reduce heat to low. Cook an additional 4 to 5 hours or until apples are tender and chicken is cooked.

To Serve: Cook noodles according to package directions. While noodles are cooking, remove chicken and cut into slices. Arrange noodles on serving platter and top with chicken. Spoon sauce and fruit over all.

Nutritional Data (based on 5 servings)

PER SERVING		EXCHANGES	
Calories	549	Milk	0.0
Fat (gm)	4.9	Veg.	0.5
Sat. Fat (gm)	1.2	Fruit	3.0
Cholesterol (mg)	91	Bread	2.5
Sodium (mg)	548	Meat	3.0
Protein (gm)	43	Fat	0.0
Carbohydrate (gm)	89		
% Calories from fat	8		

CHICKEN CREOLE

Use large chicken breasts for this New Orleans-inspired recipe, as small breasts will cook too quickly.

4-5 Servings

- 1 cup defatted chicken broth
- 1 6-oz. can tomato paste
- 1 large onion, chopped
- 2 cups chopped cabbage
- 1 large green bell pepper, seeded and diced
- 2 large garlic cloves, minced
- 1 bay leaf
- 1 tablespoon lemon juice
- 1 tablespoon Worcestershire sauce
- 1 tablespoon granulated sugar
- 2 teaspoons dried basil leaves
- 2 teaspoons Dijon-style mustard
- ¼ teaspoon black pepper
- 3-4 drops hot pepper sauce
- 2½-3 lbs. large bone-in chicken breast halves, skin and fat removed
- 1¼ cups uncooked long-grain white rice

In bottom of large slow cooker, whisk together chicken broth and tomato paste until smooth. Add onion, cabbage, green pepper, garlic, bay leaf, lemon juice, Worcestershire sauce, sugar, basil, mustard, black pepper, and hot pepper sauce. Stir to mix well. Add chicken.

Cover and cook on high 1 hour. Stir chicken into sauce. Reduce heat to low, and cook an additional 5 to 6 hours. Remove and discard bay leaf.

A half-hour before serving, cook rice according to package directions. Remove chicken. When cool enough to handle, cut into slices and discard bones. Serve individual portions of chicken and vegetables over rice.

Nutritional Data (based on 5 servings)

PER SERVING		EXCHANGES	
Calories	423	Milk	0.0
Fat (gm)	5.0	Veg.	2.5
Sat. Fat (gm)	1.3	Fruit	0.0
Cholesterol (mg)	91	Bread	2.5
Sodium (mg)	235	Meat	3.5
Protein (gm)	40	Fat	0.0
Carbohydrate (gm)	53		
% Calories from fat	11		

CHICKEN IN WINE AND MUSHROOM SAUCE

One nice feature of the Crock-Pot is that mushrooms develop a rich, hearty flavor without sauteing. Be sure to use large chicken breasts, as small ones will cook too quickly.

5-6 Servings

     1 large onion, finely chopped
     2 garlic cloves, minced
     2 large carrots, peeled and grated or shredded
     8 ozs. fresh mushrooms, sliced (generous
        2 cups)
     1 bay leaf
  4-5 large bone-in chicken breast halves, skin and
        fat removed (about 3½ lbs.)
     2 teaspoons Italian seasoning
    ¼ teaspoon dry mustard
    ½ teaspoon salt (optional)
    ¼ teaspoon black pepper
  1¼ cups red Burgundy wine
     1 6-oz. can tomato paste
     1 tablespoon Worcestershire sauce
10-12 ozs. uncooked spaghetti *or* other pasta
        Parsley sprigs for garnish (optional)

In large Crock-Pot or other slow cooker, combine onion, garlic, carrots, mushrooms, and bay leaf. Arrange chicken over vegetables. Sprinkle with Italian seasoning, mustard, salt, if desired, and black pepper.

In a small bowl, combine wine, tomato paste, and Worcestershire sauce. Stir to mix well. Pour over chicken.

Cover and cook 1 hour on high. Stir. Reduce heat to low and cook an additional 5 to 6 hours or until chicken is done. Remove and discard bay leaf.

Cook pasta according to package directions and drain well in colander. Meanwhile, cut chicken into slices and return to sauce. Spoon individual portions of sauce and chicken over pasta. Garnish with parsley sprigs, if desired.

Nutritional Data (based on 6 servings)

PER SERVING		EXCHANGES	
Calories	511	Milk	0.0
Fat (gm)	5.9	Veg.	2.0
Sat. Fat (gm)	1.5	Fruit	0.0
Cholesterol (mg)	106.7	Bread	3.0
Sodium (mg)	239	Meat	4.5
Protein (gm)	48.7	Fat	0.0
Carbohydrate (gm)	55.4		
% Calories from fat	11		

BEEF, VEGETABLE, AND BARLEY SOUP

Thick and hearty, this soup will warm you up on a cold winter day.

6-7 Servings

¾ lb. ground round of beef
1 large onion, chopped
2 large garlic cloves, minced
3 cups shredded cabbage
2 large celery stalks, sliced
2 large carrots, peeled and sliced
⅓ cup pearl barley
1 cup peeled potato cubes (¾ in.)
6 cups fat-free, reduced-sodium beef broth *or* regular defatted beef broth
2 teaspoons dried thyme leaves
1 teaspoon dried basil leaves
1 teaspoon chili powder
1 teaspoon paprika
½ teaspoon dry mustard powder
2 bay leaves
¼ teaspoon black pepper
1 14½-oz. can reduced-sodium stewed tomatoes *or* regular stewed tomatoes
Salt to taste (optional)

In Dutch oven or large skillet, combine ground beef, onion, and garlic. Cook over medium heat, stirring frequently, until beef has changed color.

Turn out meat mixture onto large plate lined with paper towels to absorb any excess fat.

In large slow cooker, combine cabbage, celery, carrots, barley, potatoes, broth, thyme, basil, chili powder, paprika, mustard, bay leaves, and pepper. Add beef and onion mixture. Cover and cook on low 7 to 9 hours or until barley is tender. Add tomatoes. Cook an additional 10 minutes. Add salt, if desired.

Nutritional Data (based on 7 servings)

PER SERVING		EXCHANGES	
Calories	176	Milk	0.0
Fat (gm)	2.2	Veg.	2.0
Sat. Fat (gm)	0.7	Fruit	0.0
Cholesterol (mg)	23.4	Bread	1.0
Sodium (mg)	118	Meat	1.0
Protein (gm)	16.2	Fat	0.0
Carbohydrate (gm)	24.3		
% Calories from fat	11		

CHUNKY CHICKEN SOUP

Here's a flavorful Italian-style chicken soup, with chunky vegetables for added texture. The rice helps thicken the broth. Be sure to use large, bone-in chicken breast halves or a whole breast since smaller pieces will cook too quickly.

5-6 Servings

1 large onion, chopped

2 celery stalks, thinly sliced

2 large carrots, peeled and thinly sliced

2 cups coarsely chopped cauliflower florets

2 very large bone-in chicken breast halves, skin removed and trimmed of all visible fat (1½-2 lbs.)

6 cups fat-free, reduced-sodium chicken broth *or* regular defatted chicken broth

2 cups cooked garbanzo beans *or* 1 15-oz. can garbanzo beans, well drained

½ cup uncooked long-grain white rice

1½ teaspoons dried thyme leaves

1 teaspoon each dried basil leaves and dried marjoram leaves

2 large bay leaves

¼ teaspoon black pepper

1 14½-oz. can stewed tomatoes

In 5-qt. slow cooker, combine onion, celery, carrots, and cauliflower. Add chicken, broth, beans, rice, thyme, basil, marjoram, bay leaves, and pepper. Cover and cook on high 1 hour. Lower heat to low and cook an additional 6 to 8 hours. Remove bay leaves and discard.

Remove chicken. When cool enough to handle, remove from bone and cut chicken into bite-sized pieces. Add stewed tomatoes to pot, and cook on high an additional 10 to 15 minutes. Return chicken to pot, and cook an additional 5 minutes.

Nutritional Data (based on 6 servings)

PER SERVING		EXCHANGES	
Calories	310	Milk	0.0
Fat (gm)	3.8	Veg.	2.0
Sat. Fat (gm)	0.8	Fruit	0.0
Cholesterol (mg)	45.7	Bread	2.0
Sodium (mg)	585	Meat	2.0
Protein (gm)	29.4	Fat	0.0
Carbohydrate (gm)	40.5		
% Calories from fat	11		

RED LENTIL SOUP

---♦---

Every supermarket in America carries brown lentils, but in many areas you have to go to a health food store to find red lentils. However, it's worth searching them out. Not only do they have a milder taste than brown lentils but the texture is finer. Since red lentils cook more quickly, they're perfect for the slow cooker.

6-7 Servings

1½ cups red lentils, sorted and rinsed
1 large onion, finely chopped
1 celery stalk, diced
1 green bell pepper, seeded and diced
1 garlic clove, minced
6 cups fat-free, reduced-sodium chicken broth *or* regular chicken broth
1 teaspoon chili powder
1 teaspoon paprika
1 bay leaf
¼ teaspoon black pepper
1½ cups reduced-fat canned or jarred spaghetti sauce
1-2 teaspoons granulated sugar (optional)

In 5-qt. slow cooker, combine lentils, onion, celery, green pepper, and garlic. Add broth, and stir to break apart lentils. Add chili powder, paprika, bay leaf, and black pepper and stir well. Cover, and cook on high 1 hour. Reduce heat to low and cook an additional 6 to 8 hours or until lentils are tender.

Raise heat to high. Stir in spaghetti sauce and continue to cook 10 to 15 minutes longer. If spaghetti sauce seems acid, add optional sugar. Remove and discard bay leaf.

Nutritional Data (based on 7 servings)

PER SERVING		EXCHANGES	
Calories	210	Milk	0.0
Fat (gm)	1	Veg.	1.0
Sat. Fat (gm)	0.1	Fruit	0.0
Cholesterol (mg)	5	Bread	2.0
Sodium (mg)	335	Meat	0.5
Protein (gm)	17	Fat	0.0
Carbohydrate (gm)	34.6		
% Calories from fat	4		

7
SALADS

I love the convenience of one-dish meals as much in the summer as in the winter. That's why I've included a chapter of hearty main-dish salads such as Curried Rice, Chicken, and Fruit Salad, Thai Pork Salad, and Confetti Turkey Salad. All of these are simple to prepare, and all feature meat or seafood combined with a variety of other ingredients, including grains, fruits, beans, vegetables, and salad greens.

In addition, the salads are tossed with easy-to-make reduced-fat dressings. Some include fat-free dairy products. Others combine oil and vinegar with chicken broth—which carries the flavor of the herbs and spices without adding much fat.

I enjoy these salads as summer luncheon or dinner entrees or to pack in picnic coolers. They also work well as part of a buffet menu any time of the year.

BULGUR AND BEEF SALAD

Traditionally, bulgur salads are vegetarian. However, I've added ground round to create a filling and flavorful main dish. Unlike most salads, this one isn't refrigerated before serving, but you do have to plan ahead. Since the bulgur isn't cooked, it's softened by soaking in hot water for three hours before the salad is assembled.

5-6 Servings

- 1 cup uncooked bulgur wheat
- ¾ lb. ground round of beef
- 1 large onion, chopped
- 1 garlic clove
- ¼ cup defatted chicken broth
- 2 tablespoons lemon juice
- 1 tablespoon balsamic vinegar
- 2 tablespoons chopped chives *or* sliced green onion tops
- 2 tablespoons fresh mint leaves *or* 1 tablespoon dried mint leaves
- 1½ teaspoons dried thyme leaves
- 1 teaspoon dried marjoram leaves
- 1 teaspoon salt, or to taste (optional)
- ¼ teaspoon black pepper
- 2-3 drops hot pepper sauce (optional)
- 1 large red bell pepper, seeded and chopped
- 2 cups chopped broccoli florets (parboiled if desired)
- 1 large fresh tomato, cubed
- 1 medium cucumber, peeled and chopped

To soften bulgur, bring 5 cups water to a boil in medium saucepan. Add bulgur and set aside for 3 hours. Drain off excess water, using a large sieve.

In medium skillet, brown ground round, onion, and garlic. Turn out meat mixture onto large plate lined with paper towels to absorb any excess fat.

In large bowl, combine broth, lemon juice, vinegar, chives, mint, thyme, marjoram, salt, if desired, black pepper, and hot pepper sauce, if desired. Stir to mix well. Stir in bulgur and ground round. Stir in red pepper, broccoli, tomato, and cucumber. Garnish with additional chives or some of the chopped tomato, if desired. Serve immediately.

Nutritional Data (based on 6 servings)

PER SERVING		EXCHANGES	
Calories	228	Milk	0.0
Fat (gm)	7.6	Veg.	2.0
Sat. Fat (gm)	2.9	Fruit	0.0
Cholesterol (mg)	36	Bread	1.0
Sodium (mg)	73	Meat	1.5
Protein (gm)	16	Fat	0.5
Carbohydrate (gm)	26		
% Calories from fat	29		

TACO SALAD

◆

This popular salad is hearty enough for a summer supper. Note that a small amount of meat goes a long way, since I've replaced some of it with bulgur wheat. The fat-free tortilla chips called for are available at health food stores and some supermarkets. Experiment to find a brand you like. Because the salsa provides such a flavorful dressing for the salad, there's no need to add any oil.

6-7 Servings

Meat Mixture

⅓ cup uncooked bulgur wheat

8 ozs. extra-lean ground round of beef

1 medium onion, chopped

1 8-oz. can reduced-sodium tomato sauce *or* regular tomato sauce

½ cup mild reduced-sodium salsa *or* regular salsa

1 16-oz. can reduced-sodium kidney beans *or* regular kidney beans, drained

1 teaspoon chili powder *or* to taste

Salad and Dressing

6 cups shredded iceberg lettuce

2 medium fresh tomatoes, cubed, divided

1 sweet red or yellow bell pepper, chopped

2 tablespoons sliced green onion

1 cup shredded reduced-fat sharp Cheddar cheese, divided

1¼ cups reduced-sodium mild salsa *or* regular mild salsa

2 cups crumbled fat-free, salt-free tortilla chips *or* regular tortilla chips

Meat Mixture: Combine bulgur wheat with 1 cup hot water. Set aside for 20 minutes.

In a large saucepan, combine ground round and onion. Cook over medium heat, stirring frequently and breaking up meat with a spoon, until browned. Turn out mixture onto a plate lined with paper towels. When fat has been absorbed, return mixture to pan.

Drain bulgur in a sieve. Add to mixture. Stir in tomato sauce, salsa, kidney beans, and chili powder. Cover and cook over low heat an additional 15 minutes, stirring occasionally. Remove pan from heat and set aside.

Salad and Dressing: In a large bowl, combine lettuce, half of tomato cubes, bell pepper, green onion, and ½ cup of cheese. Toss to mix. Add salsa and toss to coat.

To serve, arrange lettuce mixture on individual serving plates. Mound meat mixture in center of each lettuce bed. Sprinkle tortilla chips in a circle around meat mixture. Garnish with reserved cheese and tomato cubes.

Nutritional Data (based on 7 servings)

PER SERVING		EXCHANGES	
Calories	269	Milk	0.0
Fat (gm)	4.8	Veg.	2.0
Sat. Fat (gm)	1.6	Fruit	0.0
Cholesterol (mg)	24.3	Bread	2.0
Sodium (mg)	584	Meat	1.0
Protein (gm)	17.7	Fat	0.5
Carbohydrate (gm)	39.4		
% Calories from fat	16		

THAI PORK SALAD

The idea for this unusual but very tasty dish came from a Thai restaurant in Santa Barbara. However, I've modified the recipe to increase the carbohydrates. Rice sticks are thin oriental rice noodles and can be purchased in many specialty markets. If they're unavailable, you could substitute vermicelli or angel hair pasta.

5-6 Servings

Noodles

    4 ozs. uncooked rice sticks

Dressing and Pork

    3 tablespoons reduced-sodium soy sauce, divided

    3 tablespoons dry sherry

    2 tablespoons fat-free, reduced-sodium chicken broth *or* regular defatted chicken broth

    1 tablespoon rice vinegar, divided

    2½ tablespoons sesame oil

    2 teaspoons granulated sugar

    1 teaspoon ground ginger

    2-3 drops hot oil *or* hot pepper sauce

    ½ lb. boneless "quick fry" pork loin chops, trimmed of all fat, cut into paper-thin strips

    ¼ teaspoon black pepper

    ⅛ teaspoon salt (optional)

Salad

    1½ cups cooked black beans *or* 1 15-oz. can black beans, rinsed and well drained

    1 large fresh tomato, diced

    1 8-oz. can sliced water chestnuts, drained, cut into strips

    1 large cucumber, peeled, seeded, and sliced

    1 large red bell pepper, seeded, diced

    ¾ cup coarsely chopped fresh cilantro

    2 tablespoons thinly sliced green onion tops

    5-6 cups shredded iceberg lettuce

Noodles: Cook rice sticks according to package directions until *al dente*. Rinse and cool in a colander under cold running water; cut long strands into 2-inch lengths with a scissors or sharp knife. Set aside to drain.

Dressing and Pork: In a large salad bowl, combine soy sauce, sherry, broth, vinegar, oil, sugar, ginger, and hot oil. Stir to mix well.

Place pork in a non-stick skillet coated with non-stick vegetable cooking spray. Sprinkle with 2 tablespoons of dressing mixture, black pepper, and salt, if desired. Toss to coat. Cook over medium-high heat, turning several times, until cooked through, about 4 minutes. Transfer pork and any pan juices back to dressing mixture. Stir to coat.

Salad: Add black beans, tomato, water chestnuts, cucumber, bell pepper, cilantro, and green onion to dressing. Stir to mix well. Stir in rice noodles. Refrigerate 1 hour, stirring occasionally, or up to 6 hours before serving.

To serve, stir salad mixture. Place about 1 cup lettuce on individual plates. Top with salad mixture. Garnish with additional cilantro sprigs, if desired.

Nutritional Data (based on 6 servings)

PER SERVING		EXCHANGES	
Calories	313	Milk	0.0
Fat (gm)	9.9	Veg.	2.0
Sat. Fat (gm)	2.1	Fruit	0.0
Cholesterol (mg)	18	Bread	2.0
Sodium (mg)	304	Meat	1.0
Protein (gm)	15	Fat	1.5
Carbohydrate (gm)	40.4		
% Calories from fat	28		

CHICKEN, PASTA, AND ARTICHOKE SALAD

Artichokes and tarragon are the important flavoring ingredients in this tasty chicken and pasta salad. As with many of the other salads in this chapter, the amount of fat is reduced significantly by using defatted chicken broth in the dressing.

5-6 Servings

- 1 lb. boneless, skinless chicken breast halves
- 2 teaspoons dried tarragon leaves, divided
- ¼ teaspoon salt, or to taste (optional)
- ⅓ cup defatted chicken broth
- 3 tablespoons olive oil
- 2 teaspoons lemon juice
- 1½ teaspoons dried tarragon vinegar
- ¼ cup chopped fresh chives *or* thinly sliced green onion tops
- ¼ cup finely chopped fresh parsley leaves
- ¼ teaspoon dry mustard
- ¼ teaspoon white pepper
  Dash cayenne pepper (optional)
- 1 14¾-oz. jar water-packed artichoke heart quarters, well drained
- 2 cups cubed fresh tomatoes
- 2½ cups medium-sized pasta such as cut fusilli, cooked according to package directions and well drained

Cut chicken into small bite-sized pieces, trimming off any fat. Sprinkle with ½ teaspoon tarragon and salt, if desired. In large, non-stick spray-coated skillet, cook chicken pieces over medium heat, turning frequently with large wooden or plastic spoon, 7 to 10 minutes or until they begin to brown and are cooked through. Set aside.

In large serving bowl, combine broth, oil, lemon juice, vinegar, chives, parsley, remaining tarragon, mustard, white pepper, and cayenne pepper, if desired. Stir to mix well.

Add reserved chicken, artichoke hearts, and tomatoes; stir to mix well. Add fusilli and stir to mix well.

Cover and chill 2 or 3 hours, stirring occasionally, to allow flavors to blend. Salad can be made a day ahead and refrigerated until needed.

Nutritional Data (based on 6 servings)

PER SERVING		EXCHANGES	
Calories	335	Milk	0.0
Fat (gm)	9.3	Veg.	2.0
Sat. Fat (gm)	1.5	Fruit	0.0
Cholesterol (mg)	31	Bread	2.0
Sodium (mg)	136	Meat	2.0
Protein (gm)	20	Fat	1.0
Carbohydrate (gm)	44		
% Calories from fat	25		

CURRIED RICE, CHICKEN, AND FRUIT SALAD

This flavorful salad makes a nice addition to a summer buffet table. Or serve it as a supper entrée.

6-7 Servings

Dressing

- ¼ cup reduced-fat mayonnaise
- ½ cup non-fat buttermilk
- 3 tablespoons non-fat dry milk powder
- 2 teaspoons mild curry powder, or to taste
- ½ teaspoon salt *or* to taste (optional)
- ¼ teaspoon white pepper

Salad

- 1 lb. boneless, skinless chicken breast meat, trimmed of all fat
- 1 15¼-oz. can juice-packed pineapple tidbits, well drained
- 2¼ cups cooked long-grain white rice
- 1 large red bell pepper, seeded and cubed (if unavailable, substitute green bell pepper)
- 1½ cups green seedless grapes
- 2 tablespoons sliced green onion tops

Dressing: Place mayonnaise in large serving bowl. Gradually whisk in buttermilk. With large spoon, stir in non-fat milk powder, curry powder, salt, if desired, and pepper.

Salad: Cut or tear each breast half into 2 or 3 large pieces. Place chicken pieces in medium-sized pot. Cover with 1 inch of water, and bring to a boil. Cover pot, reduce heat, and simmer 10 to 13 minutes or until chicken is cooked through. Cool chicken in colander under cold running water. Dry with paper towels, cut into bite-sized pieces, and reserve.

Drain pineapple in colander. Stir pineapple into dressing mixture. Add rice, reserved chicken, red pepper, grapes, and green onions to bowl with salad dressing. Toss to coat well. Cover and refrigerate several hours, stirring occasionally. Garnish with additional chopped green onions, if desired.

Nutritional Data (based on 7 servings)

PER SERVING		EXCHANGES	
Calories	226	Milk	0.0
Fat (gm)	4	Veg.	0.5
Sat. Fat (gm)	0.8	Fruit	1.0
Cholesterol (mg)	30	Bread	1.0
Sodium (mg)	63	Meat	1.5
Protein (gm)	13	Fat	0.0
Carbohydrate (gm)	35		
% Calories from fat	16		

COUSCOUS AND CHICKEN SALAD

Like rice, couscous makes a wonderful base for a hearty salad. Since this Middle-Eastern wheat product absorbs a lot of liquid, the dressing features a half cup of chicken broth, which carries the essence of the herbs and other flavorful ingredients without adding extra fat.

6 Servings

1 cup uncooked couscous
1 lb. boneless, skinless chicken breast meat, trimmed of all the fat and cut into bite-sized pieces
½ teaspoon salt, (optional)
¼ teaspoon black pepper
2 tablespoons olive oil
½ cup defatted chicken broth
1 tablespoon balsamic vinegar
1 tablespoon lemon juice
1 large stalk celery, thinly sliced
3 tablespoons chopped chives *or* sliced green onion tops
½ cup finely chopped fresh parsley leaves
1½ teaspoons dried marjoram leaves
1½ teaspoons dried thyme leaves
½ teaspoon salt, or to taste (optional)
¼ teaspoon black pepper
2-3 drops hot pepper sauce
2 cups cooked garbanzo beans *or* 1 15-oz. can garbanzo beans, washed and drained
1 large fresh tomato, chopped
1 cup chopped zucchini
¼ cup dark raisins

Cook couscous according to package directions. Set aside for 10 minutes.

Meanwhile, in non-stick, spray-coated skillet, sprinkle chicken with salt, if desired, and pepper. Cook chicken pieces over medium heat, turning frequently, 6 or 8 minutes or until they begin to brown and are cooked through. Remove and set aside in medium-sized bowl.

In large bowl or serving dish, combine oil, broth, vinegar, lemon juice, celery, chives, parsley, marjoram, thyme, salt, pepper, and hot pepper sauce. Stir to mix well.

Stir in reserved couscous, and coat with dressing. Add beans, tomato, zucchini, and raisins; stir to mix well. Stir in reserved chicken. Cover and refrigerate several hours, stirring occasionally, or up to 24 hours before serving.

Nutritional Data

PER SERVING		EXCHANGES	
Calories	412	Milk	0.0
Fat (gm)	8.4	Veg.	0.5
Sat. Fat (gm)	1.2	Fruit	0.5
Cholesterol (mg)	31	Bread	3.5
Sodium (mg)	108	Meat	1.5
Protein (gm)	25	Fat	1.0
Carbohydrate (gm)	60		
% Calories from fat	18		

CHICKEN AND MIXED GRAINS SALAD

Colorful, filling, and distinctive, this salad features a pleasing combination of several grains. If wild rice is unavailable, brown rice may be substituted. The grains are all cooked in one pot, but since they vary greatly in cooking time, they're added sequentially. Be sure the water returns to boiling after each addition. Also, if you have a brand of wild rice that needs to cook for an hour, lengthen the cooking time slightly.

6-7 Servings

- 1 medium onion, chopped
- ½ cup uncooked wild rice, rinsed and drained
- 1 bay leaf
- ⅓ cup uncooked orzo
- 1 cup frozen yellow corn kernels
- 1 lb. boneless, skinless chicken breast meat, fat removed, and cut into 2-in. strips
- ½ teaspoon salt (optional)
- ¼ teaspoon black pepper
- 1 teaspoon chili powder

1 16-oz. jar mild salsa
2 tablespoons olive oil
2 tablespoons mild honey (such as clover)
2 cups cooked black beans *or* 1 15-oz. can black
   beans, washed and drained
1 large tomato, cubed
2 cups lettuce, finely shredded
1 large cucumber, peeled and cubed

In a large, heavy pot, bring 3 qts. water to a boil. Add onion, wild rice, and bay leaf. Cover, reduce heat slightly, and boil 30 minutes. Add orzo, re-cover, and boil an additional 14 minutes. Add corn. Re-cover and boil an additional 4 minutes. Remove and discard bay leaf.

While grains are cooking, sprinkle chicken strips with salt, if desired, pepper, and chili powder. In large, non-stick, spray-coated skillet, cook chicken over medium heat, turning once or twice, until cooked through and slightly browned. Remove, cover, and refrigerate until salad is assembled.

Meanwhile, in large serving bowl, stir together salsa, olive oil, and honey. Set aside.

In colander, rinse grains under cold running water. Drain well. Transfer to bowl with salsa dressing and toss. Add beans, tomato, lettuce, and cucumber and stir to mix well. Cover and refrigerate 2 hours, or up to 24 hours, before serving.

To serve, arrange salad on large serving platter. Lay chicken strips over salad. If desired, garnish with sweet red bell pepper rings or parsley sprigs.

Nutritional Data (based on 7 servings)

PER SERVING		EXCHANGES	
Calories	278	Milk	0.0
Fat (gm)	5.7	Veg.	1.0
Sat. Fat (gm)	1.0	Fruit	0.0
Cholesterol (mg)	26	Bread	2.0
Sodium (mg)	607	Meat	1.5
Protein (gm)	18	Fat	0.5
Carbohydrate (gm)	40		
% Calories from fat	18		

CONFETTI TURKEY SALAD

You don't have to limit yourself to rice or pasta when it comes to main-dish salads. You can make this filling and flavorful entrée in a snap since the grains cook very quickly. And the deli-style smoked turkey called for requires no preparation beyond cutting.

5-6 Servings

1 cup water
1 small onion, chopped
½ cup uncooked couscous
½ cup quartered sun-dried tomatoes
½ cup uncooked orzo
1½ cups frozen yellow corn kernels
8 asparagus spears, washed, trimmed, and cut into 1-in. lengths
2 tablespoons olive oil
⅔ cup fat-free chicken broth
1 tablespoon balsamic vinegar
2 teaspoons lemon juice
3 tablespoons chopped chives *or* sliced green onion tops
1½ teaspoon dried basil leaves
1 teaspoon dried thyme leaves
½ teaspoon salt, or to taste (optional)
¼ teaspoon black pepper
2-3 drops hot pepper sauce (optional)
1 6-oz. package deli-style smoked turkey breast, cut into thin strips

In medium saucepan, bring water to a boil. Add onion and couscous. Cover, reduce heat, and boil 2 minutes. Remove pot from heat, stir in tomatoes, and allow to stand 10 to 15 minutes.

In Dutch oven or similar pot, bring 2 quarts water to a boil. Add orzo and cook 8 minutes. Add corn and cook an additional 3 minutes. Add asparagus and cook and additional 2 minutes, until orzo is tender. Rinse and drain ingredients well in colander.

In large bowl, combine oil, broth, vinegar, lemon juice, chives, basil, thyme, salt, if desired, pepper, and hot pepper sauce, if desired. Add reserved couscous mixture and stir to mix well. Stir in orzo and vegetable mixture and turkey. Cover and refrigerate 2 or 3 hours, or up to 12 hours, before serving, stirring occasionally.

Nutritional Data (based on 7 servings)

PER SERVING		EXCHANGES	
Calories	262	Milk	0.0
Fat (gm)	4	Veg.	2.0
Sat. Fat (gm)	0.8	Fruit	0.0
Cholesterol (mg)	11.6	Bread	2.0
Sodium (mg)	427	Meat	1.0
Protein (gm)	13.7	Fat	0.5
Carbohydrate (gm)	41.5		
% Calories from fat	18		

MARINATED TUNA AND POTATO SALAD

If you like salad Niçoise, you'll like this zesty tuna-potato salad.

5-6 Servings

1 lb. red-skinned potatoes (about 4 medium), cut into ¼-in. slices
2 tablespoons canola oil *or* safflower oil
2 tablespoons fat-free chicken broth
2 teaspoons balsamic vinegar
1 large stalk celery, thinly sliced
3 tablespoons chopped red onion
¼ cup finely chopped fresh parsley leaves
¾ teaspoon dried marjoram leaves
¾ teaspoon dried thyme leaves
½ teaspoon Dijon-style mustard
¼ teaspoon salt, or to taste (optional)
  Pinch white pepper
1 7-oz. can water-packed tuna, drained and flaked
1 large fresh tomato, chopped
1 large cucumber, peeled, seeded, and sliced into crescents
  Chopped parsley for garnish (optional)

Combine potatoes and enough water to cover in medium-sized saucepan. Cover pan and bring to boil. Reduce heat and simmer 8 to 12 minutes or until potatoes are tender but not soft when pierced with fork.

When potatoes are cooked, transfer to colander and cool slightly under running water. Drain well.

Meanwhile, in medium-sized bowl or serving dish, combine oil, broth, and vinegar. Stir to mix. Add celery, onion, parsley, marjoram, thyme, mustard, salt, if desired, and pepper. Stir to mix well.

Add potatoes, carefully stirring with large spoon to coat with dressing mixture. Be careful not to break up potatoes. Carefully stir in tuna, tomato, and cucumber. Cover and refrigerate several hours, stirring occasionally, to allow flavors to blend.

Garnish with additional parsley, if desired.

Nutritional Data (based on 7 servings)

PER SERVING		EXCHANGES	
Calories	161	Milk	0.0
Fat (gm)	5.6	Veg.	1.0
Sat. Fat (gm)	0.5	Fruit	0.0
Cholesterol (mg)	6	Bread	1.0
Sodium (mg)	142	Meat	1.0
Protein (gm)	10	Fat	0.5
Carbohydrate (gm)	20		
% Calories from fat	30		

DEVILED CRAB SALAD

◆

This wonderful combination of crab and vegetables makes an elegant luncheon entrée. Note that seasoned stuffing mix is used as a substitute for croutons since it's lower in fat.

5-6 Servings

- 1 tablespoon olive oil
- 3 tablespoons fat-free chicken broth
- 2 tablespoons chopped fresh chives *or* sliced green onion tops
- 1½ tablespoons Dijon-style mustard
- 2 teaspoons Worcestershire sauce
- 1 tablespoon lemon juice
- ¼ teaspoon (scant) salt, or to taste (optional)
- 1 teaspoon dried thyme leaves
- ⅛ teaspoon ground celery seed
- ⅛ teaspoon white pepper
- 2-3 drops hot pepper sauce
- 1 lb. fresh crabmeat, picked over and flaked
- 2 cups frozen yellow corn kernels, cooked according to package directions and well drained

2 large fresh tomatoes, seeded and chopped
1 large green bell pepper, seeded and chopped
1 cup seasoned cube-style stuffing mix
  Lettuce leaves
  Additional chopped tomato, for garnish
  (optional)

In large bowl, combine oil, broth, chives, mustard, Worcestershire sauce, lemon juice, salt, if desired, thyme, celery seed, white pepper, and hot pepper sauce. Stir to mix well. Add crabmeat, corn, tomatoes, green pepper, and stuffing mix. Toss to coat.

Refrigerate ½ to 3 hours. Serve individual portions over lettuce leaves. Garnish with additional chopped tomato, if desired.

Nutritional Data (based on 6 servings)

PER SERVING		EXCHANGES	
Calories	175	Milk	0.0
Fat (gm)	4.1	Veg.	0.0
Sat. Fat (gm)	0.6	Fruit	0.0
Cholesterol (mg)	40	Bread	1.0
Sodium (mg)	962	Meat	2.0
Protein (gm)	18	Fat	0.0
Carbohydrate (gm)	19		
% Calories from fat	20		

SHRIMP, PASTA, AND VEGETABLE SALAD

5-6 Servings

Pasta

  1½ cups uncooked fusilli *or* similar pasta shape

Dressing

  ¾ cup ketchup
  ½ cup non-fat ricotta cheese
  3 tablespoons reduced-fat mayonnaise
  1½ teaspoons prepared horseradish
  1 teaspoon lemon juice
  1 teaspoon chili powder

Shrimp and Vegetables

  1 lb. ready-to-serve medium shrimp
  1½ cups zucchini cubes
  10 cherry tomatoes, halved
  2 large celery stalks, sliced
  2 tablespoons chopped fresh chives *or* sliced
    green onion tops

To Serve

  Iceberg *or* other lettuce leaves
  Cherry tomato halves and chopped parsley for
  garnish (optional)

Pasta: Cook according to package directions. Cool under cold running water. Drain well in colander and reserve.

Dressing: Combine ketchup, ricotta, mayonnaise, horseradish, lemon juice, and chili powder in food processor container. Process, stopping and scraping down sides of container once or twice, until mixture is well blended. Transfer to large bowl.

Shrimp and Vegetables: Stir shrimp, reserved pasta, zucchini, tomatoes, celery, chives into dressing. Cover and refrigerate several hours until flavors are well blended.

To Serve: Line large serving platter with lettuce leaves and mound salad on top. Or serve individual portions on lettuce leaves. Garnish with cherry tomato halves and parsley, if desired.

Nutritional Data (based on 6 servings)

PER SERVING		EXCHANGES	
Calories	257	Milk	0.0
Fat (gm)	3.5	Veg.	1.0
Sat. Fat (gm)	0.6	Fruit	0.0
Cholesterol (mg)	152	Bread	2.0
Sodium (mg)	498	Meat	2.0
Protein (gm)	23	Fat	0.0
Carbohydrate (gm)	34		
% Calories from fat	12		

RAVIOLI SALAD

If you're on the lookout for new and tasty main dish salad ideas, give this one a try.

5-6 Servings

1 9-oz. package reduced-fat cheese ravioli
⅓ cup fat-free chicken broth
2 tablespoons olive oil
2 teaspoons lemon juice
1½ teaspoons apple cider vinegar
¼ cup chopped fresh chives *or* thinly sliced green onion tops
¼ cup finely chopped fresh parsley leaves
2 tablespoons chopped fresh *or* 2 teaspoons dried basil leaves
1 teaspoon dried thyme leaves
¼ teaspoon dry mustard
¼ teaspoon white pepper
Dash cayenne pepper (optional)
½ teaspoon salt, or to taste (optional)
1 14¾-oz. jar water-packed artichoke heart quarters, well drained
1 cup cooked, *or* canned, cannellini beans
2 cups cubed fresh tomatoes
1½ cups diced zucchini
½ red bell pepper, seeded and diced
1 celery stalk, diced

Cook ravioli according to package directions. Rinse and drain in colander. Reserve.

In large serving bowl, combine broth, oil, lemon juice, vinegar, chives, parsley, basil, thyme, mustard, white pepper, and cayenne pepper and salt, if desired. Stir to mix well.

Add ravioli, artichoke hearts, beans, tomatoes, zucchini, red pepper, and celery and stir to mix well.

Cover and chill in refrigerator 2 or 3 hours, stirring occasionally, to allow flavors to blend. Salad can be made a day ahead and refrigerated until needed.

Nutritional Data (based on 6 servings)

PER SERVING		EXCHANGES	
Calories	180	Milk	0.0
Fat (gm)	6.0	Veg.	2.5
Sat. Fat (gm)	1.9	Fruit	0.0
Cholesterol (mg)	2.2	Bread	1.0
Sodium (mg)	339	Meat	0.0
Protein (gm)	7	Fat	1.0
Carbohydrate (gm)	27		
% Calories from fat	28		

8

QUICK-AND-EASY MEALS

In today's hectic world, there are always days when you need to get dinner on the table in a hurry. One alternative is to stop on the way home from work for a bucket of chicken or a pizza. That may be the speedy solution, but it's likely to be the high-fat, high-sodium solution as well.

In this chapter I've collected some of my answers to the quicker dinner crisis: soups, hearty sandwiches, and skillet dinners that are good for you and easy to prepare. And they all cook in less than half an hour. Some take advantage of the microwave to speed preparation. Most use convenience foods such as dairy-case ravioli, salsa, shredded cheese, and canned beans. There's even a flavorful cheese and vegetable soup that gets its creamy texture from frozen mashed potatoes.

SAUSAGE, POTATO, AND BELL PEPPER SKILLET

*My family loves this easy skillet dinner, which takes
advantage of the microwave to partially cook the potatoes
and soften the sun-dried tomatoes.*

4 Servings

- 5 cups (1¼ lbs.) peeled (or unpeeled) thinly sliced red potatoes
- ½ cup dry-packed sun-dried tomatoes
- ¾ cup fat-free, reduced-sodium chicken broth *or* regular chicken broth, divided
- 4 cups frozen mixed red, green, and yellow bell peppers with onions
- 4 ozs. turkey *or* other low-fat sausage, diced
- 1 teaspoon dried thyme leaves
- 1 teaspoon dried marjoram leaves
- ¼ teaspoon salt (optional)
- ⅛ teaspoon black pepper

Place potatoes in a medium-sized microwave-safe bowl. Top with tomatoes.
Pour ¼ cup of broth over all. Cover with wax paper, and microwave on
high power 4 minutes. Remove tomatoes to a cutting board. Stir potatoes
and microwave an additional 3 minutes or until almost tender. Set aside.

Meanwhile, cut up any large pieces of onion in bell pepper-onion mixture.
Also cut tomatoes into quarters. In a 12-inch non-stick skillet, combine
tomatoes, bell pepper-onion mixture, sausage, thyme, marjoram, salt, and
pepper with ¼ cup broth. Cook over medium-high heat, stirring frequently,
until onions are tender and sausage is cooked, 5 or 6 minutes.

Add reserved potatoes to skillet along with remaining broth. Cook, uncovered, an additional 5 or 6 minutes until flavors are blended and broth is
somewhat reduced.

Nutritional Data

PER SERVING		EXCHANGES	
Calories	255	Milk	0.0
Fat (gm)	3.1	Veg.	3.0
Sat. Fat (gm)	0.6	Fruit	0.0
Cholesterol (mg)	18	Bread	2.0
Sodium (mg)	450	Meat	0.5
Protein (gm)	12.6	Fat	0.0
Carbohydrate (gm)	48.8		
% Calories from fat	10		

QUICK BACON AND PASTA SKILLET

---◆---

I like to make this easy dinner with half an 8-ounce package of Canadian bacon and freeze the remaining bacon for another meal. The recipe is very flexible. Although I've called for zucchini and/or cauliflower, you could substitute broccoli and sweet red bell peppers for a tasty variation.

4 Servings

- 8 ozs. (2½ cups) uncooked penne *or* similar pasta shape
- 4 ozs. Canadian bacon, cut into thin strips
- 2 teaspoons olive oil
- 1 medium onion, chopped
- 2 garlic cloves, minced
- 1 14½-oz. can reduced-sodium stewed tomatoes *or* regular stewed tomatoes
- 2 cups sliced zucchini *or* cauliflower florets *or* a combination of the two
- 2 teaspoons Italian seasoning
  Salt (optional) and pepper to taste

Cook pasta according to package directions. Drain and rinse.

Meanwhile, in a large non-stick skillet, combine bacon, oil, onion, and garlic. Cook over medium heat, stirring frequently, until onion is tender, 5 or 6 minutes. Add tomatoes, zucchini or cauliflower, and Italian seasoning and stir to mix. Bring to a boil, cover, and reduce heat. Season to taste with salt and pepper, if desired. Simmer 6 to 7 minutes, stirring occasionally, or until vegetables are tender.

Stir in pasta.

Nutritional Data

PER SERVING		EXCHANGES	
Calories	325	Milk	0.0
Fat (gm)	5.6	Veg.	2.0
Sat. Fat (gm)	1.2	Fruit	0.0
Cholesterol (mg)	13.5	Bread	3.0
Sodium (mg)	380	Meat	1.0
Protein (gm)	15.2	Fat	0.0
Carbohydrate (gm)	53.7		
% Calories from fat	16		

CHICKEN AND PASTA WITH SUN-DRIED TOMATO SAUCE

Here's a high-flavor, quick-cooking chicken skillet dinner. Cooking the vegetables in the microwave speeds the preparation.

5 Servings

½ cup fat-free, reduced-sodium chicken broth *or* regular defatted chicken broth
2 teaspoons olive oil
1 medium onion, chopped
½ cup dry-packed sun-dried tomatoes, quartered
1 teaspoon dried basil leaves
¼ teaspoon dried thyme leaves
1 teaspoon granulated sugar
¼ teaspoon salt (optional)
1 lb. boneless, skinless chicken breast halves, trimmed of all fat, and cut into bite-sized pieces.
¼ teaspoon salt (optional)
¼ teaspoon black pepper
1 15-oz. can reduced-sodium tomato sauce *or* regular tomato sauce
2½ cups (8 ozs.) uncooked fusilli *or* similar pasta shape, cooked according to package directions
Chopped chives *or* parsley for garnish (optional)

In a 2-cup measure or similar microwave-safe bowl, mix broth, oil, onion, sun-dried tomatoes, basil, thyme, sugar, and, if desired, salt. Cover with wax paper, and microwave on high power 2 minutes. Stir. Microwave an additional 2 minutes. Remove from microwave and set aside.

Meanwhile, sprinkle chicken with salt, if desired, and pepper. In a non-stick skillet coated with non-stick spray, cook chicken pieces over medium-high heat, stirring frequently until they are cooked through and begin to brown, 7 to 8 minutes. When chicken pieces are done, stir in tomato sauce and sun-dried tomato mixture. Bring to a boil, reduce heat, and simmer 10 to 12 minutes until flavors are well blended. Stir in cooked pasta.

Garnish with chopped chives or parsley leaves, if desired.

Nutritional Data

PER SERVING		EXCHANGES	
Calories	361	Milk	0.0
Fat (gm)	5.2	Veg.	2.0
Sat. Fat (gm)	1	Fruit	0.0
Cholesterol (mg)	55.2	Bread	2.5
Sodium (mg)	221	Meat	2.5
Protein (gm)	29.2	Fat	0.0
Carbohydrate (gm)	48.2		
% Calories from fat	13		

TURKEY WITH APRICOTS AND CHILIES

---♦---

This quick and easy recipe proves that leftover turkey doesn't have to be boring. The tangy combination of chilies and apricots is reminiscent of an Indian chicken dish.

4-6 Servings

1¼ cups uncooked long-grain white rice
2 teaspoons non-diet, tub-style margarine *or* butter
1 cup chopped onion
2 garlic cloves, minced
1¼ cups defatted chicken broth, divided
1 teaspoon ground cumin
¼ teaspoon ground coriander
⅛ teaspoon ground allspice
10 dried apricots, quartered
1 tablespoon chopped canned green chilies
1 cup chopped fresh tomato
1 lb. cooked turkey breast meat, cut into bite-sized pieces
Dried apricot slices for garnish (optional)

Cook rice according to package directions.

Combine margarine, onion, garlic, and 2 tablespoons of broth in Dutch oven or similar large pot. Cook over medium heat, stirring frequently, until onion is soft, about 5 or 6 minutes. If liquid begins to evaporate, add a bit more broth.

Stir in cumin, coriander, and allspice. Add remaining broth, apricots, chilies, and tomato. Stir to mix well. Reduce heat, cover, and simmer 10 minutes or until flavors are well blended.

Stir in turkey and cook an additional 5 minutes.

Serve individual portions of turkey mixture over rice. Garnish with apricot strips, if desired.

Nutritional Data (based on 6 servings)

PER SERVING		EXCHANGES	
Calories	319	Milk	0.0
Fat (gm)	2.6	Veg.	0.0
Sat. Fat (gm)	0.7	Fruit	0.5
Cholesterol (mg)	65	Bread	2.0
Sodium (mg)	260	Meat	3.0
Protein (gm)	27	Fat	0.0
Carbohydrate (gm)	46		
% Calories from fat	7		

RAVIOLI AND FRESH VEGETABLES

Crisp, fresh vegetables make a wonderful counterpoint to the ravioli in this skillet dinner. Use 1 or 2 quick-cooking vegetables such as small broccoli or cauliflower florets, diced zucchini, sliced carrot, or chopped red or green bell pepper. Or, for convenience, buy a package of precut vegetables in the supermarket produce department.

4 Servings

1 medium onion, diced
2 garlic cloves, minced
5 cups vegetables for stir-fry (see headnote)
3 tablespoons dry sherry
2 teaspoons Italian seasoning
2 teaspoons extra-virgin olive oil
1 9-oz. package reduced-fat cheese ravioli
1 15-oz. can reduced-sodium tomato sauce *or* regular tomato sauce
Salt (optional) and pepper to taste

In a 12-inch non-stick skillet, combine onion, garlic, vegetables, sherry, Italian seasoning, and olive oil. Toss to mix well. Cook over medium-high heat, stirring frequently, 7 to 8 minutes or until vegetables are almost tender.

Meanwhile, cook ravioli according to package directions. Rinse and drain in a colander.

Stir tomato sauce into vegetable mixture. Reduce heat and cook, uncovered, an additional 2 or 3 minutes, stirring frequently. Stir in ravioli, and cook an additional 1 minute. Add salt, if desired, and pepper.

Nutritional Data

PER SERVING		EXCHANGES	
Calories	193	Milk	0.0
Fat (gm)	4.1	Veg.	3.0
Sat. Fat (gm)	0.9	Fruit	0.0
Cholesterol (mg)	3.8	Bread	1.0
Sodium (mg)	207	Meat	0.5
Protein (gm)	9.5	Fat	0.5
Carbohydrate (gm)	28.4		
% Calories from fat	19		

ORANGE PORK

Orange juice and cloves give this easy dish a rich flavor.

4-5 Servings

1 lb. quick-fry sliced pork loin, trimmed of all fat and cut into thin strips
¼ teaspoon salt (optional)
⅛ teaspoon black pepper
2 teaspoons olive oil
3 cups frozen mixed red, green, and yellow bell peppers and onions
1½ cups orange juice, divided
2 teaspoons granulated sugar
1 teaspoon dried thyme leaves
¼ teaspoon ground cloves
1¼ cups uncooked long-grain white rice, cooked according to package directions

Sprinkle pork with salt, if desired, and pepper. In a large, non-stick skillet coated with non-stick spray, cook pork over medium heat until white on both sides, 3 to 4 minutes. Remove from pan, and set aside in a medium bowl.

Add oil, bell pepper-onion mixture, and 2 tablespoons of orange juice to skillet, and cook over medium-high heat, stirring occasionally, until onion is tender, 3 to 4 minutes. If liquid begins to evaporate, add a bit more juice. Stir in remaining juice.

Add reserved pork, sugar, thyme, and cloves. Stir to mix well. Bring to a boil. Cover, lower heat, and simmer 12 minutes. Remove cover, raise heat slightly, and simmer an additional 6 to 8 minutes until sauce has cooked down and thickened.

Serve pork and vegetables over rice.

Nutritional Data (based on 5 servings)

PER SERVING		EXCHANGES	
Calories	428	Milk	0.0
Fat (gm)	10.8	Veg.	2.0
Sat. Fat (gm)	3.1	Fruit	0.5
Cholesterol (mg)	42.4	Bread	2.5
Sodium (mg)	50	Meat	3.0
Protein (gm)	25.5	Fat	0.0
Carbohydrate (gm)	57.3		
% Calories from fat	23		

OPEN-FACED GREEK SANDWICHES

———————◆———————

These quick open-faced sandwiches taste best when made with Greek-style non-pocket pita bread and are eaten with a knife and fork.

4 Servings

1 cup mixed frozen red, green, and yellow bell peppers and onions

1 15-oz. can chick peas, rinsed and drained

2 cups small cauliflower florets

1 15-oz. can reduced-sodium tomato sauce *or* regular tomato sauce

1 garlic clove, minced

¾ teaspoon dried thyme leaves

2-3 drops hot pepper sauce (optional)

1½ ozs. (about ⅓ cup) chopped feta cheese

4 Greek-style non-pocket pita breads

Preheat broiler.

If necessary, cut up any large pieces of onion in bell pepper-onion mixture. In a medium-sized pot, combine peppers and onions, chick peas, cauliflower, tomato sauce, garlic, thyme, and hot pepper sauce, if used.

Bring to a boil. Reduce heat and simmer 10 to 12 minutes until flavors are blended.

Meanwhile, place pita bread on a baking sheet, and very lightly toast on one side.

To serve, place pitas on individual plates. Spoon one-fourth of chick pea mixture over each pita. Sprinkle each with one-fourth of feta cheese.

Nutritional Data

PER SERVING		EXCHANGES	
Calories	378	Milk	0.0
Fat (gm)	6.2	Veg.	2.0
Sat. Fat (gm)	2.1	Fruit	0.0
Cholesterol (mg)	9.4	Bread	4.0
Sodium (mg)	927	Meat	0.0
Protein (gm)	16.5	Fat	1.0
Carbohydrate (gm)	68.9		
% Calories from fat	14		

BEEF AND BEAN BURRITOS

♦

*This fast and spicy Mexican sandwich has become a family
favorite. Combining ground turkey breast with the ground round
substantially reduces the fat content of the dish. Cooked with
the beef, the turkey takes on a beefy flavor.*

6 Servings

8 ozs. ground round of beef
4 ozs. ground turkey breast
2 garlic cloves, minced
1 16-oz. jar reduced-sodium mild salsa *or* regular
   mild salsa
1 15 oz. can reduced-sodium tomato sauce *or*
   regular tomato sauce
1 16-oz. can reduced-sodium kidney beans *or*
   regular kidney beans, drained and mashed or
   lightly chopped in a food processor
1½ teaspoons chili powder
1 teaspoon granulated sugar
6 6-in. flour tortillas
¾ cup (3 ozs.) shredded reduced-fat Cheddar
   cheese

In a Dutch oven or similar large pot, combine ground round, ground
turkey, and garlic. Cook over medium heat, stirring frequently until beef
has browned, 4 or 5 minutes. If meat begins to stick, add a bit of water.

Add salsa, tomato sauce, kidney beans, chili powder, and sugar. Bring to a
boil. Cover, reduce heat, and simmer 15 to 18 minutes, stirring frequently,
until flavors are blended. Remove from heat.

Meanwhile, warm tortillas in oven or microwave according to package
directions. To serve, lay each tortilla flat on a plate. Fill with ⅙ of meat-
bean mixture. Sprinkle with ⅙ of cheese. Fold over and serve.

Nutritional Data

PER SERVING		EXCHANGES	
Calories	326	Milk	0.0
Fat (gm)	6.6	Veg.	2.0
Sat. Fat (gm)	2	Fruit	0.0
Cholesterol (mg)	33.2	Bread	2.0
Sodium (mg)	765	Meat	2.0
Protein (gm)	22	Fat	0.5
Carbohydrate (gm)	42.9		
% Calories from fat	19		

EASY TORTILLA SOUP

---◆---

Non-fat tortilla chips add crunch and texture to this flavorful soup.

6 Servings

8 ozs. ground round of beef
2 cups chopped onions
3¾ cups reduced-sodium, defatted beef broth *or*
   regular beef broth
1 16-oz. jar reduced-sodium mild salsa *or* regular
   mild salsa
1 16-oz. can reduced-sodium kidney beans *or*
   regular kidney beans, well drained
1½ cups frozen corn kernels
1 teaspoon chili powder
2 cups crushed no-sodium, non-fat baked tortilla
   chips *or* regular non-fat baked tortilla chips
   Salt to taste (optional)
½ cup (2 ozs.) grated reduced-fat Cheddar
   cheese

In a Dutch oven or similar large, heavy pot, combine ground round and onions. Cook over medium heat, stirring frequently, until beef is browned, 5 to 6 minutes.

Add broth, salsa, beans, corn, and chili powder. Stir to mix. Bring to a boil. Reduce heat, and simmer 15 to 20 minutes.

Stir in tortillas, and simmer an additional 5 minutes. Stir in salt to taste, if desired.

To serve, sprinkle each bowl of soup with cheese.

Nutritional Data

PER SERVING		EXCHANGES	
Calories	280	Milk	0.0
Fat (gm)	3.9	Veg.	2.0
Sat. Fat (gm)	1.1	Fruit	0.0
Cholesterol (mg)	23.3	Bread	2.0
Sodium (mg)	622	Meat	1.5
Protein (gm)	20	Fat	0.0
Carbohydrate (gm)	42		
% Calories from fat	12		

RED AND WHITE BEAN AND BACON SOUP WITH PASTA

With canned beans and Canadian bacon, you can have a hearty bean and bacon soup on the table in minutes.

7 Servings

6 ozs. Canadian bacon, cut into small strips
1 large onion, chopped
2 large celery stalks, minced
2 teaspoons olive oil
6 cups fat-free, reduced-sodium chicken broth *or* regular chicken broth, divided
1 18-oz. can cannellini beans, rinsed and drained
1 15-16-oz. can reduced-sodium red kidney beans *or* regular kidney beans, drained
1 15-oz. can reduced-sodium tomato sauce *or* regular tomato sauce
2 teaspoons Italian seasoning
3 ozs. (½ cup) uncooked orzo

In a Dutch oven or similar large pot, combine bacon, onion, celery, oil, and ¼ cup broth. Cook over medium heat, stirring frequently, 6 to 7 minutes or until onion is tender. Add remaining broth, beans, tomato sauce, and Italian seasoning. Bring to a boil over high heat. Add orzo.

Reduce heat and boil gently, uncovered, stirring frequently, until flavors are blended and pasta is tender, 18 to 20 minutes.

Nutritional Data

PER SERVING		EXCHANGES	
Calories	257	Milk	0.0
Fat (gm)	4	Veg.	2.0
Sat. Fat (gm)	0.8	Fruit	0.0
Cholesterol (mg)	11.6	Bread	2.0
Sodium (mg)	771	Meat	1.0
Protein (gm)	20.6	Fat	0.0
Carbohydrate (gm)	40.3		
% Calories from fat	13		

INDEX